GCSE
Success

REVISION GUIDE

Business Studies

Bro

Neil Denby

Contents

The Business Studies examination that you are taking will be provided by one of five different examination boards. These are AQA, OCR, Edexcel, CCEA or WJEC. You must make sure that you know the examination board for which you are entered. This is important because, although all examination boards test the same content, some consider certain parts to be more important than others, so they put more emphasis on them.

The 'specification' is the list of content on which you will be examined. This, and a description of how you will be examined, can be found online by visiting the website of your examination board.

You can also find past papers to give you an idea of how questions will be asked and marked (these are also useful for practice).

The websites of the examination boards are:
www.aqa.org.uk/
www.ocr.org.uk/
www.edexcel.com/
www.rewardinglearning.org.uk/ (CCEA)
www.wjec.co.uk

Examination questions will test you in four different ways:
- Some questions will test your **knowledge**. You may just have to show that you can remember a fact or define a term.
- Some questions will test your **application**. You will be given an example of a business with which to work. This could be given to you in advance, or it could be part of the examination paper. It is usually called a **case study**. Marks are earned for how well you link your answer to the case study.
- Some questions will test your ability to make comparisons and weigh up alternatives. This is called **analysis**. You will need to look at both

sides of an argument, or at the positive and negative points of two opposing views or possibilities. Make sure that you don't waste time by repeating yourself. Candidates often say, for example, that 'an advantage would be that customers get more choice' and a disadvantage is that 'customers might not get more choice'.
- Finally, some questions carry higher marks as they will test your ability not only to make decisions and judgements but to say why you have made them. This is called **evaluation**.

Some examination boards will use simple **knowledge** questions, such as multiple choice or short definitions. Others will want you to apply your knowledge in order to gain marks.

At the end of each section in this book there are test questions so that you can have a go at answering all the different types of question that may be used. Again, though, you must check which ones are going to be most important to you and your examination board.

You will often be asked to make a decision, or to judge between two possible alternatives. Remember that there are usually no marks for making a decision. The marks are for the reasons you can give to support the decision that you make.

Always make sure that any decisions or reasons that you give are clearly linked to the business that you have been given to study. Many marks are lost by candidates suggesting actions or ideas that are not appropriate to a business because of its size, its customers or its market.

Don't forget that you may also have coursework, or 'controlled assessment' to complete, so some of your learning may be tested in this way rather than through an examination.

Starting a Business Enterprise

What a Business Is

People need certain goods and services in order to survive. To begin with, they need food, clothing and shelter. Later, as society develops and becomes more complex, they want other goods and services. A **need** is something people require for survival (like food and water). A **want** is any other good or service. Businesses are started by people who aim to provide these goods and services for customers. If they sell the right products, at the right price, they will succeed. People who start businesses take on risks but gain the reward of **profit** – the surplus of revenue over costs. Such people are called **entrepreneurs**.

Why Businesses Are Set Up

In most cases, a business is set up to make a profit. Sometimes, though, a business aims to provide a service to a community for reasons other than making a profit. These are called **social enterprises** and they are often charities or co-operatives.

A successful business understands both its customers and its **market**. A market is anywhere that a buyer and seller come together to agree on a sale. Buyers demand products; businesses supply them. **Supply and demand** work together to decide on the price of a product. To succeed, a business needs a unique selling point (USP) – something that only it can offer.

Businesses provide new products which offer innovative approaches like this Smart Car

✓ Maximise Your Marks

In business studies, you can often use the knowledge you have from your own experience to help in the exam. Think about these questions:

- Who is competing against whom in your local town centre or shopping mall? Are there two burger bars, for example, or two cinemas? What is it that makes you use one rather than the other?
- How can businesses compete if they do not compete on price? Most will try to compete by adding value to the sales process. This could be through better quality, convenience or good design. Recognisable brands are also seen as adding value as they keep customers loyal.
- What was the last major purchase you made? Whom did you buy it from? Why from that business and not somewhere else? This will give you a good way to describe added value and how it worked for you.

How Businesses Compete

There will usually be a number of businesses operating in a market, all in **competition** with each other. Businesses need to know about competition. They can find out about the market and can build **competitor profiles** to better help them compete. Successful businesses know how to compete by adding **value**. They make sure that customers receive better value for money than from the competition. Some ways to add value are through:

- better service
- convenience (such as a good location or a delivery service)
- providing different ways for customers to pay
- being efficient
- providing special design features.

Gaps in the Market

New businesses will look for a **gap in the market**. This is where a demand for a good or service exists but is not currently being met by an existing business. A **market map** can be used to see where there are gaps. Businesses with new products or ideas may be able to create a gap in the market so that people want the products that they have for sale. This is often achieved through **advertising**.

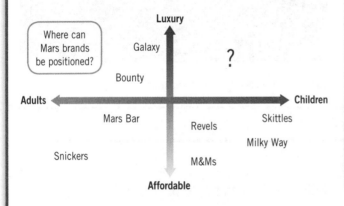

✓ Maximise Your Marks

- You should be able to explain how a business can create a gap in a market with a new product. Think about new technology for your examples.
- If your examination gives you a case study to use, you must make sure that your answers use examples from it to support the points that you make. If it does not, you should be able to come up with examples of your own.
- Remember that you should be able to explain that the most important part of any business transaction is the customer. It is essential that a business keeps its customers happy and coming back time and again.

? Test Yourself

1. Explain the difference between a 'want' and a 'need'.
2. Give three examples of how a business can compete through added value.
3. Which of your examples do you think is most important, and why?
4. Why would a business build a competitor profile?

★ Stretch Yourself

1. Give the main reason why anyone would set up a business.
2. Define 'social enterprise'.
3. Explain what is meant by a 'gap in the market'.

Enterprise and Entrepreneurs

Enterprise

'**Enterprise**' is the term used to describe when a person takes a business risk in order to gain a possible **reward**. In business terms, this reward is the profit made by the business. People with enterprise skills are called **entrepreneurs**.

Entrepreneurs carry the risk of starting a business and they provide its **organisation**. They take risks to bring new or different products and processes to the market.

New businesses often fail, but entrepreneurs will still want to try out new ideas or new products. This willingness to keep trying is one of the key reasons behind successful entrepreneurs.

The three key parts that lead to successful enterprises are:
- **invention** – the creation of new goods, services and processes (e.g. mobile phones)
- **innovation** – bringing in new methods of marketing, production, distribution, etc. (e.g. Apple computers)

- **protection** – using patent and copyright laws to stop competitors copying ideas (e.g. as James Dyson has done).

Sir Richard Branson – A successful entrepreneur

Entrepreneurial Skills

Entrepreneurs need a special set of skills to succeed. They need to reduce the risks of their enterprise through good planning and by researching both customers and competitors. Key enterprise skills include:
- **teamwork** – both leading and being part of a team
- **organisation** – planning skills and setting priorities
- **problem solving** – being able to think through a problem
- **networking** – using other people's skills, knowledge and expertise
- **energy** – the enthusiasm to keep going
- **communication** skills – explaining ideas clearly and persuasively
- **keeping an overview** – the ability to make connections and see the whole picture.

Entrepreneurs and enterprise are the key to business success, especially to new businesses. Entrepreneurs bring not only new products but new ideas on how to market them and how to satisfy the customer. Successful entrepreneurs keep trying. Many have lived through numerous failures before finally succeeding.

💡 Boost Your Memory

Entrepreneurs use creative skills to help them succeed. See if you can be creative with a mnemonic for the key skills of an entrepreneur. TOP NECK could help you remember the list opposite, or you could make a rhyme or rap of your own.

Creative Thinking

Entrepreneurs need to be **creative thinkers**. New ideas can be generated through taking a deliberate decision to think creatively. Deliberate creativity means making a conscious effort to be creative. This is a powerful way of trying out new business ideas. It can help to encourage business innovation. The entrepreneur uses his or her own knowledge and skills, plus the facts about a situation, to try to solve a problem. Sometimes this is through lateral thinking. This means thinking 'outside the box' – looking for new and unusual solutions to problems.

'What If?' Scenarios

Entrepreneurs need to be able to calculate and manage risk. They need to judge what actions they may need to take in the future. They can use 'what if?' scenarios to do this. This is when an entrepreneur asks a question such as: 'What if a new competitor entered the market?' or 'What if my main supplier folded?' or 'What if the Government increased tax on the product?'

Possible outcomes, or 'scenarios', can then be worked through to predict what might happen and to have a solution to any problems waiting.

Computer software such as spreadsheets can be used in order to model 'what if?' scenarios. Modelling of this kind is used by big and small businesses to predict everything from a small price rise to global climate change.

Using computer spreadsheets for 'what if?' scenarios

✓ Maximise Your Marks

- You should be able to explain how thinking 'outside the box' can create competitive advantage for a business and use examples to back up your explanations.
- What new products or innovations have recently come to the market? Explain how these are different.
- Remember to think about how you could be creative in your own ideas if you were setting up your own business. What would be new or original about your business that would attract customers?

? Test Yourself

1. Define what is meant by 'enterprise' and its reward.
2. What is meant by an 'entrepreneur'?
3. What are the three key parts of a successful enterprise?
4. What is meant by deliberate creativity?

★ Stretch Yourself

1. List the key skills possessed by entrepreneurs.
2. What is meant by a 'what if?' scenario?
3. Explain how computers can help with such scenarios.

Stakeholders

Stakeholders

Stakeholders are those people, groups or organisations that have a **stake**, or **interest**, in the performance of a business. They are the people who use the business, who work for the business, who supply the business, who regulate the business, who compete against the business and who own the business. They are the people in the **communities** where the business operates. Businesses can only exist if entrepreneurs take **risks** on new products or in new markets. The owners carry most of the risk, so they have a stake in how well the business performs. **Stakeholder groups** are either internal or external groups.

Local community

✓ Maximise Your Marks

In business studies, you can often use your own experience to help you remember key facts. Think about those businesses that you buy from; those that operate near your home, school or college; those that your parents work for, or that you might work for now or in the future. You are a stakeholder yourself in a number of businesses.

Stakeholder Conflicts

Sometimes competing stakeholder groups have different aims that bring them into conflict with each other.

A customer

Some examples include when owners may want higher profits but customers want lower prices; or when suppliers want to be paid at once but owners want time to pay.

It is often necessary to balance both sides of the argument and then come to a decision on how best to resolve it, such as borrowing money to pay suppliers now.

Internal Stakeholders

Many stakeholder groups have a direct interest in the **success** of the business. These are called **internal stakeholders**, and they include the owners and employees of the business. In a small business, the owner may be a single person (**sole trader**), or a small group of people (**partnerships, cooperatives**). Larger businesses, such as companies, have **shareholders** who own the business. Each owns part of the business and receives a **share** of any profits that the business makes.

Employees want the business to provide good working conditions and fair pay. **Managers** are the employees who help to run the business. Their pay may be linked to the success of the business.

Internal stakeholders are also called **direct stakeholders**. They have a direct interest in the success of the business.

External Stakeholders

External stakeholders have a less direct stake in a business than internal stakeholders. These groups include customers, suppliers, banks, the government, pressure groups and the communities in which the business operates.

Each has different priorities:
- Customers want quality and reliability.
- Suppliers want to sell their products and be paid.
- Banks and other financial stakeholders have lent or given the business money and want a return on this.
- Government needs businesses to operate within the law and to pay taxes.

- The community may want the business for some reasons, such as jobs, but not want it because of other factors such as pollution.

External stakeholders may also be called **indirect stakeholders**, but they can still have a big influence on the business.

The Influence of Stakeholders

Stakeholders can both be influenced **by** a business and have an influence **on** the business:
- Owners aim for success and profit and can influence a business through **investment**, **expansion** or **new ideas**. Owners decide what to sell and in which markets.
- Employees can influence the business by doing a good job (or have a negative influence if they do a poor job).
- Managers take day-to-day decisions in the running of the business.

- Customers can choose to buy from the business or not.
- Suppliers are responsible for the quality and reliability of supply.
- Government influences business through legislation and taxation.
- **Pressure groups** try to bring about change.

⚡ Boost Your Memory

You must always remember to think of the two ways that stakeholders and businesses are connected. They have an influence **on** the business and are influenced **by** the business.

✓ Maximise Your Marks

Higher level candidates need to understand that stakeholders do not always take decisions that are good for the business. Many groups have their own stakeholders to please. Banks, for example, may take decisions – such as refusing a loan – that are in their own interests rather than those of the business.

❓ Test Yourself

1 What is a stakeholder?
2 Why are internal stakeholders also called direct stakeholders?
3 Define what is meant by external stakeholders.
4 Give three examples of external stakeholders.

★ Stretch Yourself

1 Give an example of a possible stakeholder conflict.
2 Suggest a possible solution to this conflict.
3 Give three examples of stakeholder groups and explain what each might want from a business.

Setting Business Aims and Objectives

Measuring Progress

Aims and **objectives** are the ways in which a business measures the progress it is making.

Businesses need to know whether they are succeeding. Aims say what the business wants to achieve in the long run. They are key to how the business operates. Objectives are shorter term. **Progress** can be measured by reaching objectives and then setting new ones.

Many businesses set **SMART** targets. These are *Specific, Measurable, Achievable, Realistic* and *Time-related*.

For a small business, the main types of aim will be personal or non-financial – such as **survival**, **job satisfaction** and **independence**. For larger businesses, aims may include **profitability**, **growth**, **competing** effectively and increasing market share.

Setting Business Aims

Aims are long-term goals towards which the business can work. They are often not very precise, and the business may never be able to reach them. Aims like 'being the best in the world' or 'being first choice for everyone' may often be found in **mission statements** or vision statements.

The aims of a **start-up** business are going to be very different to those of an established, growing business. The main aim for a start-up business is likely to be survival. This may involve **breaking even** (when all costs are covered by revenues). Other aims may be wider and harder to measure,

such as **customer satisfaction**, a good **reputation** and **loyalty** from suppliers and customers.

The final aim may be a long way away

Starting a Business

There are numerous advantages and disadvantages of setting up a business, but there are factors other than money that might be important. Such factors include the independence of working for yourself, for example, or the pleasure of job satisfaction – of knowing that this is 'a job well done'.

It is always important to have the right aims for the right type of business.

Objectives are stepping stones used to reach the aims of a business. Each objective achieved puts the business one step closer to its aims.

Objectives are targets on the way to reaching an aim

Wider Aims

Businesses may have wider aims, such as operating **ethically** and **sustainably**.

Acting ethically means 'doing the right thing' – for example, not using child labour or causing pollution.

Acting sustainably is an environmental aim. Businesses should try to take no more out of the environment than it replaces. Sustainability aims use objectives linked to, for example, renewable energy, recycling and creating less waste and pollution.

Some businesses have the aim of helping others, or of sharing profit in a fair way. Some of these are called charities or co-operatives. They are still run as businesses, but their aims reflect why they were set up, so a charity might have the aim of raising as much as possible for sick children.

Companies have usually found that being ethical and environmentally aware is actually very good for business. Firstly, some ideas save money, such as recycling and renewable energy. Secondly, people prefer to buy from a business that they think treats people and the environment fairly.

Renewable energy sources help businesses to meet environmental aims

Using Aims and Objectives to Plan

A **business plan** shows how a business might reach its aims. It describes the methods, staff and products it intends to use to try to achieve them. It will include financial details and forecasts. It is often used as a tool for raising finance.

A good business plan lays down the direction that the business will take and outlines aims and objectives. It is a working document for the business and a management tool to be updated at regular intervals. New businesses can reduce the risk of failure through using a good business plan.

✓ Maximise Your Marks

- If you were going to the bank for a loan for your business, what do you think it would want to know? This is the information that would go on a business plan.
- To reach higher marks, you will need to explain the difference between aims and objectives and give relevant examples from the business that you are studying. Always put your answer in the context of this business to show how it uses its aims and objectives to measure and drive progress.

❓ Test Yourself

1. Outline what is meant by an aim.
2. Why might some aims never be reached?
3. What does SMART stand for?
4. What is likely to be the main aim of a start-up business?

⭐ Stretch Yourself

1. How are objectives related to aims?
2. Describe the factors other than money that can be important to a person setting up a business.
3. Give some examples of things that might be included in a business plan.

Business Location

Where to Locate a Business

One of the most important decisions that an entrepreneur has to make is where a business will be **based**. All businesses, even the smallest ones, need somewhere from which to operate. Even a tiny business selling goods or services via the Internet needs somewhere to plug in the computer!

An important factor is the product or market that the business is in. A business may:
- deal directly with customers, in which case it must be close to them
- need display and storage space plus parking or public transport for customers
- need good transport and distribution if it operates nationally.

There are government grants and other packages of assistance to help businesses set up in certain areas. The EU also provides regional assistance.

The ideal location for a business will not be too expensive, but will help to attract customers.

Different businesses will have different needs. For example, a business may need a large or specialist **labour force**, or may need to be close to customers to provide personal services.

Businesses may locate close to competitors, to encourage customers to 'shop around'. They may also gain from the reputation of some parts of the country – Sheffield steel, for instance. Some businesses are '**footloose**', in that they can locate anywhere. **E-commerce** allows customers to see stock and buy online, so their actual location is less important.

Locating Growing Businesses

If a business grows, it may need to change its location to keep costs down and increase revenues. A larger business may need more space for operations, storage and transport. It may need better links to **infrastructure** such as water, power and communications.

If it expands overseas, it must decide whether to sell from the UK or set up abroad. Costs abroad could be lower, but there could also be issues such as different languages and laws. A business that locates overseas must obey local laws and conduct business in the language and currency of the host country.

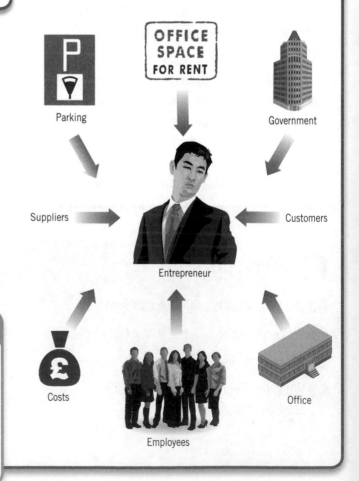

✓ Maximise Your Marks

Remember, if asked about location, that many businesses have been established for a long time and the original reason for them being there may have gone. On the other hand, a new business can decide to put itself in exactly the most favourable spot.

Location and Stages of Production

Location may depend on where the business sits in the **chain of production**. There are usually three clear stages of production:

- Raw materials have to be extracted or mined in the **primary** sector.
- The **secondary** sector involves manufacturing and processing these materials.
- The **tertiary** sector contains services such as distribution, retail, banking, communications and insurance.

Primary businesses need to be near the source of raw materials, to keep the cost of transporting them as low as possible. For tertiary businesses, location is unimportant if they can deliver the service (such as insurance or banking) from anywhere. A secondary business needs to know whether closeness to customers or to raw materials, is more important.

Boost Your Memory

It's as easy as 1, 2, 3. Primary (think of your first school) is raw materials; secondary (your second school) is manufacture and processing; tertiary (third stage or higher education) is services.

More Location Factors

For secondary businesses, a key location factor may be the cost of transport, linked to whether it is a **bulk decreasing** business or a **bulk increasing** business.

Bulk decreasing means that products become easier or cheaper to transport after processing or manufacture, so the business needs to be near raw materials.

If it is a bulk increasing industry, such as wood being turned into furniture, it needs to be located near its market.

Businesses are 'pushed' or 'pulled' towards locations, like being on an elastic band. Nearer to markets may be better for customers, but may mean higher costs and rents. Nearer to raw materials may lower some costs but may be too far from customers. Businesses must strike a balance.

✔ Maximise Your Marks

For top marks, you must show that you can analyse (weigh up both sides of an argument) and judge (come to a decision). There is not always a right or wrong answer so, when asked to compare two locations for a business, you should weigh up the good and bad points of each, make a decision, and then explain how you have reached this decision (justification).

？ Test Yourself

1. Explain why the type of business is a key factor in its location.
2. List three important location factors.
3. What is a 'footloose' business?
4. Give the three stages of production.
5. What might be a key factor in the location of a business in the primary sector?

★ Stretch Yourself

1. What is meant by 'bulk increasing' and 'bulk decreasing' businesses?
2. What problems might result from relocating a business overseas?

Practice Questions

 Complete these exam-style questions to test your understanding. Check your answers on page 90. You may wish to answer these questions on a separate piece of paper.

Knowledge Questions

Answer questions 1–10 first, then read the case study before answering the other questions. Each knowledge question is worth 1 mark. For these questions, put a ring around the letter of the correct answer.

1 The factor that makes your business stand out is called the:

a) unique sticking point b) unique sticking place c) unique selling point d) unique selling place.

2 Profit is defined as the surplus of:

a) revenue over costs b) costs over sales c) costs over revenue d) stock over sales.

3 Which of the following does not represent 'value added'?

a) convenience b) profit c) quality d) gift wrapping.

4 A bulk increasing industry needs to locate:

a) near its market b) near a port c) near a railway d) near raw materials.

5 Which of the following is not an external stakeholder?

a) customers b) employees c) the Government d) communities.

6 Aims are:

a) short-term goals b) long-term goals c) short-term targets d) long-term targets.

7 The ideal location for a business may depend on whether it sells goods or:

a) makes clothes b) grows food c) provides services d) sells products.

8 A business providing personal services needs to be located:

a) on an industrial estate b) near customers c) near technology d) near raw materials.

9 A business extracting raw materials will be located:

a) on the high street b) near customers c) near technology d) near raw materials.

10 Service providers need to locate close to:

a) shops b) markets c) raw materials d) technology.

Case Study

Josh and Mary have decided that they would like to combine their skills to start a business. Josh is a good photographer and has had pictures that he has taken displayed in various exhibitions. He would like to use his skills to earn an income. Mary worked in a sales department but now wants to be her own boss. She is also very good at mounting photographs in albums and attractive frames.

The two friends intend to set up a business taking photographs at weddings, christenings and other family events, which they will then present ready mounted in an album. The best photograph at each event will be provided mounted and framed. The business will be called Snapz.

Application Questions

11 Who are the internal and external stakeholders in Snapz? (4)

....

....

....

12 i) Explain what you think Josh and Mary's aims are likely to be at the time of the business start-up.

ii) How do you think that these will change if the business grows? (6)

....

....

....

....

....

....

13 Describe the unique selling point (USP) of Snapz and how it is adding value to the business. (4)

....

....

....

Analysis and Evaluation Questions

Josh thinks that the new business should have a set of high profile offices on the high street, with window display space in order to attract customers. Mary thinks that, at least to start with, the business should locate somewhere that is low-cost and they should try to sell via the Internet, but this would mean having to advertise the service. She thinks the costs on the high street are too high.

14 Analyse which of the two location options you would advise Josh and Mary to take. (8)

....

....

....

....

....

....

....

How well did you do?

| 0–8 | Try again | 9–16 | Getting there | 17–24 | Good work | 25–32 | Excellent! |

Structuring a Business

Legal Structures for Businesses

A business can decide to operate as one of a number of **legal structures**. These are divided into:
- those with a few owners or even a single owner
- those with many owners.

A small business, especially a start-up, is limited to being a **sole trader**, a **partnership** or a **private limited company**. The smallest is the 'one person' business, called the sole trader.

Partnerships are agreements between two or more people.

Private limited companies have a small number of shareholders and cannot sell shares to the public. They are often family concerns.

All businesses have to have some sort of legal standing, but owners don't necessarily have to do anything official. If you buy and sell on eBay, for example, you are a sole trader; if you agree to do so with someone else, you are a partnership. No formal agreement or paperwork is necessary.

The legal status of a business is likely to change as it expands, and can often be guessed from its name. 'Harold Smith, Grocer' will be a sole trader; 'Sellem & Floggit, Estate Agents' will be partners. The type of business may also give clues – sole traders are often service providers or retailers, while partnerships are often of professional people.

Advantages and Disadvantages

Sole traders gain from being independent. The owner has control of the business, makes all the decisions and keeps any profit or suffers any loss. Owners raise the finance themselves, from personal sources or by borrowing. Raising more money is often hard, so expanding the business may be difficult.

Partnerships benefit from shared responsibility and more expertise. Partners share the responsibilities, organisation, workload and profits (or losses). However, partners may disagree and this can harm the business. The joint owners receive any profit and share risk equally unless a Deed of Partnership states otherwise.

Extra stakeholders, such as shareholders in a private limited company, can mean disagreements.

Hairdresser

✔ Maximise Your Marks

Students often make the mistake of saying that sole traders 'have to do all the work themselves'. Remember that just because a sole trader is a 'one person business', this does not mean that they can't employ people or take holidays. Some sole traders are quite large, with several managers and employees.

Tax and Legal Issues

Sole traders and partnerships are easy and cheap to set up, with no formal paperwork needed. Each pays personal **income tax** and **National Insurance** (the 'tax' that covers the health service and state pensions). They will need to fill in a tax return each year. Their accounts do not have to be made public, but must be accurate for tax reasons.

Private companies must be established in law and registered at **Companies House**. They must produce accounts and make them available to the public. They must also tell the tax authorities that they exist, and must pay a tax on their profits. If turnover is large enough, they must register for **VAT** (Value Added Tax).

Liability

Liability is the legal term used for the **responsibility** of the owners of a business for the **debts** of that business. It can be either **limited** or **unlimited**. Sole traders and partnerships have unlimited liability. Owners are personally responsible for all the debts of the business. This means that if the business cannot pay its debts, the owner's personal money and possessions can be seized. Private or public limited companies have limited liability. This means that the responsibility for business debt is limited to the amount of money invested in the business.

In the UK, **private limited companies** are usually shortened to '**Ltd**' and **public limited companies** are usually shortened to '**plc**'. These letters are placed after the name of the company as an indication to others that this company has limited its liability.

Having limited liability can actually be a disadvantage to a business. Having 'plc' or 'Ltd' in the name is actually a warning to stakeholders that this business may not be able to pay its debts. Banks may be less likely, therefore, to lend to limited companies without guarantees of some sort.

Liability is the responsibility for the debts of the business

✓ Maximise Your Marks

If you are aiming for higher marks, remember that for sole traders and partnerships, the tax issues are the same as for an individual, as the income they receive is personal income. They are effectively working for themselves and are usually described as 'self-employed'. Company profits are different, and are treated differently by the tax authorities.

❓ Test Yourself

1. What is a sole trader?
2. What is a partnership?
3. What is a private limited company?
4. Explain what you have to do to set up as a sole trader.
5. How would you recognise that a business is a company?

⭐ Stretch Yourself

1. Explain what is meant by limited liability.
2. Explain how stakeholders are warned about limited liability.
3. How can having limited liability be a disadvantage to a business?

Larger Business Organisations

Public Limited Companies

Private limited companies can raise money by becoming **public limited companies**. The business offers its **shares** for sale to the public via the **stock exchange**. A stock exchange listing means anyone can buy shares, including **competitors**. Competitors who buy shares have information about the business, but also have a say in how it is organised or operated.

Shareholders have one vote per share, so they can affect the decision-making process. Public company shareholders may be more interested in gaining a quick **profit** than in the long-term health of the business, so they may buy and sell shares regardless of the strength of the business.

You can see a list of the top companies, and the price of their shares, in most daily newspapers. Many factors – including the health of the company – push the price of shares up and down.

Becoming a plc is not complicated, and it is a good way for a company to raise large amounts of finance. It is only really suitable for larger private companies, though, as it involves producing evidence that the business is in good health and reliable. Businesses produce a document (called a **prospectus**) showing the accounts of the business and that it is profitable and has a good future.

Becoming a plc is called 'floating' a company on the stock exchange.

Disadvantages of plcs

Share prices are reported publicly

Becoming a plc does have some disadvantages. For example, it is necessary to provide **reports** each year, which include details of finances and profits as well as the company's performance for the year. These reports are free and they have to be made accessible to anyone who requests them; often they are available online.

All of the company's strengths and weaknesses can be seen, even by competitors. This can give competitors a good idea of what is happening with certain businesses.

Public Sector Businesses

The public sector refers to those businesses owned not by the public but by local or national government on behalf of the public. Some are public corporations. These may exist because an industry has been **nationalised**, which means they have been taken from private ownership into the public sector. Others may never have been in the private sector but have been set up originally by government. These include the BBC (set up with a charter).

At one time, most of the major industries in the country were publicly owned, including coal, shipbuilding, iron and steel, water, gas and telecommunications. Most have now been sold into private hands.

The Government can take businesses into public ownership because they think this will be in the public interest. This applies not only to areas like defence contracts and nuclear power plants, but also to key businesses in the economy. When some banks were collapsing in 2008 due to poor management, the Government took them into public ownership.

Social Enterprises

The Eden Project – an example of a social enterprise

Most businesses try to make a profit. In some special cases, businesses have social aims, so are called **social enterprises**. Social aims bring benefits to stakeholder groups such as communities, employees and customers. There are often ethical and moral reasons for social enterprises. Business owners want to be fair and not exploit suppliers, workers or customers. Ethical practice is doing the right, or moral, thing.

There are many social enterprises such as charities, voluntary groups, cooperatives and even community-owned enterprises.

There are also voluntary groups that provide a service to the community. Examples include St John's Ambulance and the Lifeboat Service.

These groups may be supported by charitable donations. Charities try to raise as much money as possible for their particular cause.

✔ Maximise Your Marks

To get the best marks, it's worth remembering that:
- The public sector is not just nationalised industries, but includes all services provided by national and local government, including the National Health Service and Education. This makes it a very large and important part of the economy.
- Social enterprises usually look to maximise the social and ethical aims of the business, rather than profits – but if they make profits, they will share them fairly and use them to support social aims.

❓ Test Yourself

1 What is a public limited company?

2 Give one disadvantage of selling shares to the public.

3 Outline what you would find in a prospectus.

4 What is the public sector?

⭐ Stretch Yourself

1 Outline the information a plc must supply to the public.

2 Explain why this can be a disadvantage to the plc.

3 What is a social enterprise?

Franchising

Franchises

A **franchise**, or franchising, is a way for a successful business to expand and for other businesses to share in that success. A successful business can expand by selling other businesses the right to set up using its ideas, **brands** and **promotions** and, perhaps most importantly, its **business model**.

Pizza Hut franchises out its delivery service in the UK

For the business buying the franchise, this is a way of starting, owning and operating a business without the high levels of risk that may be associated with other types of start-up. The business model is already successful, so chances of failure are reduced. For the business selling the franchise, it is a safe way to expand.

There are two important parts to a franchise:
- The **franchiser** is the seller of the franchise that has a successful product, brand or format. Franchisers provide ideas, support, training, advertising and a strong and successful brand. In turn, they gain from expanding their brand or idea and also from fees made by the franchisee.
- The **franchisee** is the business that buys into the success of the established business. It buys the use of its name, its brand, its advertising, its reputation and its support.

Franchisers charge a fee for the franchise and collect a **royalty**, based on a percentage of the annual sales of the franchisee. Because a franchisee is buying into a successful product, the fee for the franchise can often be quite high and there can be a lot of competition to buy a franchise.

Franchises as Companies

A franchise is not a form of business ownership but a type of business organisation. Both franchiser and franchisee can be sole trader, partnership or limited company, although it is more likely that the franchiser will be a company than the franchisee.

A franchiser might not want a franchisee to be a limited company because limited liability might put its investment at risk.

💡 Boost Your Memory

Think of words like 'employer' and 'employee' to make sure that you get 'franchiser' and 'franchisee' the right way round. The one selling the franchise is the 'franchis**er**' and the one buying it the 'franchis**ee**', in the same way that the employ**er** employs and the employ**ee** is the one who is employed.

Buying or Selling a Franchise

Franchising brings advantages (and some possible disadvantages) to both the franchiser and the franchisee. It helps the successful business selling the franchise to expand and it gives the business buying the franchise a much better chance of surviving and succeeding.

Many franchisers lay down strict rules as to what the franchisee can or cannot do, so buying a franchise can remove some of the independence of a business.

Franchising is also applied to services. For example, rail companies (like Virgin or South West Trains) buy the right to run a service on existing routes for a set time period.

UK rail companies are also franchises

Advantages and Disadvantages

The main advantage to franchisees is that they are buying into an **established** business. They will get help with products, staff, training, marketing and sales materials. The franchiser may run national **promotions** to support the brand, so the franchises are less likely to fail. Franchisees may gain an **exclusive territory** or area, away from any competitors. The disadvantage to franchisees is the lack of **independence**.

The advantage to the franchiser is that their **business model** is spread. Franchisers also receive an income from the franchisee. A possible disadvantage is that a poor franchisee could harm their **reputation**.

✔ Maximise Your Marks

- Higher level candidates will always make sure that the solution they offer to a problem is sensible for the business given. Franchising is only a sensible route if it is possible to duplicate a process or service easily.
- There are some disadvantages to a franchise linked to the franchisee's freedom to make changes or decisions – think about what you would *not* be allowed to do if you took on, say, a burger bar franchise.

❓ Test Yourself

1. What is a franchise?
2. Outline the role of the franchiser.
3. Outline the role of the franchisee.
4. Describe the main ways in which charges for a franchise are met.

★ Stretch Yourself

1. Explain why a franchise is not a form of business ownership.
2. Why might a franchiser not want a franchisee to be a limited company?
3. What could be the main disadvantages of a franchise?

Internal Organisational Structures

Centralised and Decentralised Structures

Business organisation describes the ways in which businesses are **structured** internally. Structure will depend on the business size, on the type of business or on the type of market in which it operates.

Some organisations are controlled from the centre. This means decisions are made by a few people. In an organisation that is very **centralised**, all decisions will be made at the top. This can mean quick decision-making, but could mean management is too far away from customers and does not understand them.

Decentralised organisations spread decision-making. This can mean better decisions made at local level.

Key Players in a Structure

Organisational charts show the structure of a business and the key people in it. A **family tree** type chart shows the place of managers and workers. Each manager has a **span of control**, defined as wide or narrow according to the number of workers under his or her control. The people underneath are called **subordinates** and the manager has **authority** over them. Most organisational structures are in **layers**, where the people at the top have more authority than those at the bottom. This is called a **hierarchy**. Large businesses may be split into divisions based on product type, location, or functions such as marketing.

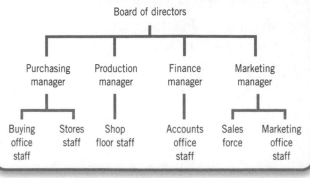

Tall and Flat Structures

Some businesses have a **tall structure**, with many layers but perhaps few people at each layer. Communication between layers tends to be formal, but can be slow.

Example of tall structure

Some businesses, on the other hand, have a **flat structure**. There are few layers and there may be many people at each layer. This means communication both within and between layers is generally good.

Example of flat structure

Organisational structures often have in-built inefficiencies because of the way a business has developed – for instance, growth may have left managers in charge of departments that are too large. Efficiency can sometimes be increased by taking out layers. This is called **delayering**.

💡 Boost Your Memory

A good way to remember how a strict hierarchy works is to think of the armed forces, where instructions are passed from top to bottom down a chain of command.

Functional Areas

All businesses have to carry out certain **functions** in order to operate. In smaller businesses like sole traders and partnerships, the owners will carry out most functions. Even in larger businesses, information technology means that managers now do a lot of administrative work. The main functions are:

- **Finance** – deals with money, accounts and the financial records of the business.

- **Human resources** – hires, trains, promotes, disciplines and fires people. It also deals with wages, salaries, retirement and pensions.
- **Marketing** – operates market research, advertising and promotion.
- **Production** – linked to the manufacture of the goods.
- **Administration** – provides all the service operations.

Communications in a Business

Clear **communication** is vital to all businesses. Communication consists of four steps: **sender**, **message**, **medium**, and **receiver**. If the right message does not get to the right person, in the right format, then the business is failing to be efficient.

Communications may be:
- internal – within the structure, or
- external – with people or bodies outside the organisation.

They may also be:
- formal – with a set format and a record kept, or
- informal, often face-to-face.

Communication may also be through different **media** – oral, written and, increasingly, electronic. Both internally and externally, many communications are now carried out via email.

Information sharing

✓ Maximise Your Marks

- Business functions are not always divided neatly into functional areas, so remember what it is that the business has to do, rather than the department where it takes place.
- Think of all the tasks that you can do on a computer. Years ago, none of these would have been done by an ordinary worker, but would have been carried out by specially trained administrative staff such as typists.

❓ Test Yourself

1. Describe a centralised organisational structure.
2. Describe a decentralised organisational structure.
3. What is meant by a hierarchy?
4. Outline the parts of a family-tree type organisational chart.
5. List the main functions that all businesses carry out.

★ Stretch Yourself

1. Explain the difference between a tall organisational structure and a flat organisational structure.
2. Explain the difference in internal communication between a tall and a flat structure.

Practice Questions

 Complete these exam-style questions to test your understanding. Check your answers on page 91. You may wish to answer these questions on a separate piece of paper.

Knowledge Questions

Answer questions 1–10 first, then read the case study before answering the other questions.
Each knowledge question is worth 1 mark. For questions 1–5, put a ring around the letter of the correct answer.

1 A small business, especially a start-up business, is limited to being any of the following except:

a) public corporation **b)** sole trader **c)** partnership **d)** private limited company.

2 A manager with just a few subordinates would be described as having a span of control that is:

a) wide **b)** thin **c)** deep **d)** narrow.

3 The person who sells a franchise is called the:

a) franchisee **b)** franchiser **c)** employer **d)** employee.

4 The person who buys a franchise is called the:

a) franchisee **b)** franchiser **c)** employer **d)** employee.

5 The initial payment made to buy a franchise is called a:

a) salary **b)** fee **c)** royalty **d)** price.

In the following questions, fill in the missing word or words.

6 A .... is a business that is owned and run by one person.

7 .... means the responsibility of the owner for the debts of the business.

8 A company that sells shares to the public is called a .... limited company.

9 A company that is taken from private ownership into the public sector has been ....

10 A business with many layers in its organisation, but few at each layer, is said to have a .... organisational structure.

Case Study

Kris has just finished his advanced driving course and is wanting to set up his own driving instructor business. His friend Matt has offered to handle advertising and marketing and to use his accountancy skills to keep the books. He would also help to pay for Kris's new car. Kris does not know whether to set up as a sole trader or a partnership.

Another option is to buy a franchise from a national driving school called UK Motor Training Ltd (UKMTL). This would cost Kris in the first instance to buy the franchise, but he would be guaranteed to get customers and would be covered by UKMTL's advertising, branding and marketing support. However, Matt thinks the amount he would have to continue to pay UKMTL for the franchise is too much.

Application Questions

11 Describe the advantages to Kris of being a sole trader. (3)

12 Describe the advantages to Kris of forming a partnership. (4)

13 Using UKMTL and Kris as an example, describe how a franchise works. (8)

Analysis and Evaluation Questions

14 Discuss whether Kris should set up as a sole trader or partnership. (6)

15 Consider whether Kris should operate as an independent or a franchisee. (5)

How well did you do?

| 0–9 | Try again | 10–18 | Getting there | 19–27 | Good work | 28–36 | Excellent! |

Understanding the Market

Market Research

Market research tells a business about its market. The business uses the information gained from research to help it succeed now and to help it to plan for the future. It is the way that businesses find out what customers want.

Market research can be divided into different categories. It can be **primary** (**field**) or **secondary** (**desk**) research.

Research may produce data that is either **quantitative** (numbers and statistics) or **qualitative** (opinions and views). Quantitative data may show trends and patterns. It is harder to analyse. Data has to be **collected**, **analysed** and **interpreted** to make it useful. This can be expensive.

Businesses can divide or '**segment**' a market so that each segment can be targeted. Common segments are age, income, lifestyle, location, sex and ethnicity.

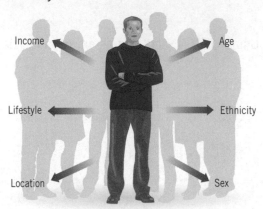

Customer Research

Businesses can find the information they need by asking customers directly or by using market data. Asking customers usually involves using **questionnaires**, **interviews**, **surveys** or **focus groups**, or just by watching customer behaviour (such as footfall counts). This is **primary research**.

Primary research is information that has not been collected before: it is 'first hand' information. It is also called 'field research'. Often, the methods of collecting primary research make it expensive, but it can be targeted and focused to collect exactly the data required by the business.

✓ Maximise Your Marks

Remember that there are many types of market research that could be used by a business, so you should know about different ways of collecting primary and secondary data and which are likely to be used by bigger and smaller businesses.

What Customers Want

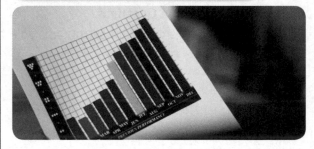

Some of the key things that businesses need to know to help them to sell their products to their customers are:
- who will buy the product and how often
- how much the customer will pay
- where the customer will buy the product from
- which other businesses are selling the product
- what can be used to persuade the customer to buy.

✓ Maximise Your Marks

It is helpful to remember that many methods of market research can be either too expensive or too difficult for a small business to carry out. Larger businesses are often in a position to get better research.

Competitor Research

Businesses also need to know about their competition. They can use market data like company reports, market reports, published resources and government statistics or the Internet. This is **secondary research** – research that has been previously published. Secondary research may be cheap (or even free – many government-collected statistics are available at www.statistics.gov.uk), but much of it may not be any use to the business.

A great deal of market data about customers and customer behaviour already exists. Some businesses, like big supermarket chains, collect huge amounts of data from customer loyalty cards. This can be used to tell them how customers behave.

A market position can be shown through a **SWOT** analysis. This measures the internal *Strengths* and *Weaknesses* of the business against its external *Opportunities* and *Threats*.

Strengths and Opportunities help it to reach its objectives, while Weaknesses and Threats hold it back. It is usual to draw up a table to show this.

SWOT	Help the business meet its objectives ⬇	Do not help the business meet its objectives ⬇
Internal to the business ➡	Strengths	Weaknesses
The external environment ➡	Opportunities	Threats

Checking Data

When using market research data from a secondary source, a business must be very careful how they handle it. Things they must consider include:

- The source – is it reliable?
- The date – is it recent?
- Who commissioned it? Is it likely to be biased?

If there are two sets of data, it is also important to ensure that they are comparing 'like with like'. If not, they may be making assumptions or interpretations based on incorrect information.

✓ Maximise Your Marks

- Always make sure that the research is right for the business you are given. Small businesses may be unable to collect large samples of questionnaires, but may find useful information for free on government websites.
- A* students need to be able to criticise the data they are given and use this in their answers and judgements. For example, research sponsored by the road haulage industry in favour of more roads may not be very reliable!

❓ Test Yourself

1. Outline the common segments used to divide a market.
2. Give three ways of collecting primary data.
3. Give three ways of collecting secondary data.
4. What is a SWOT analysis?

★ Stretch Yourself

1. What are the key things a business might want to know from its research?
2. Explain three things a business should check about a piece of secondary research before using it. Give reasons for your answer.

The Marketing Mix: Product

The Marketing Mix

The **marketing mix** is a term given to the way that a business sells a product. Successful sales (and therefore a successful business) depend on the *Product* being offered at the right *Price*, in the right *Place* and with the right *Promotion*. The marketing mix is a balance of these four areas (or '**four Ps**').

It is a key skill of the business person to maintain a balance that helps the business to increase **sales**. However, success is about more than just sales. It is also about **customer satisfaction** and **loyalty**.

The Product

Without a **product** (something to sell), the other parts of the marketing mix are of no use.

Some businesses sell a single product – one example being a taxi business, where the product is selling taxi rides. Others, such as supermarkets, sell a **range** of products.

As a business grows, it may want to expand its **product portfolio** – that is, the range of goods that it sells. The wider the range, the more different markets the business reaches.

A **branded** range helps businesses to persuade customers to be loyal and to try new products (under the same brand). It is a way of standing out from competition (called '**differentiation**').

Although a wider range helps businesses access wider markets, it does also bring other risks, such as extra costs and extra competition.

✓ Maximise Your Marks

No single part of the marketing mix is more important than the others. You should always talk about the 'balance' of the marketing mix across the four areas and recognise a marketing mix with too much emphasis on one part – for example a lot of advertising but a poor product.

The Boston Matrix

The Boston Matrix is a way to analyse a product portfolio by showing the importance of each product in one of four categories:
- *Stars* have a high market share in a fast growing – often new – market. They need a lot of **promotion**.
- *Problem children* have a small market share in a fast-growing market. They could provide profits in the future.
- *Cash cows* have a large market share of a mature market. These are established brands that do not need much spent on promotion. Often these are **market leaders**.
- *Dogs* have a small share of a slow-growing market and are often **costly** to maintain.

Managers choose to do different things with each type of product:
- Usually they keep the cash cows, using the money to support stars.
- They also keep the stars and try to turn them into cash cows.
- They spend on the problem children to turn them into stars.
- They sell off the dogs.

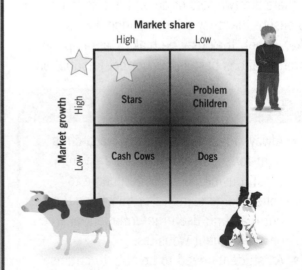

The Boston Matrix

Product Life Cycle

As demand for a product changes, it passes through a **life cycle**, starting with its **launch** and ending with its **death**. The stages are:

- development, where no sales are made, but there are costs
- launch (also called the **introduction stage**), where costs can be high as advertising is needed
- growth, which brings the risk that competitors will see the success and bring out rivals
- maturity, when many people have bought the product but there are also many competitors
- decline, when sales fall; the business must decide whether to support the product with extension strategies, or let it go to its...
- death, a withdrawal from the market.

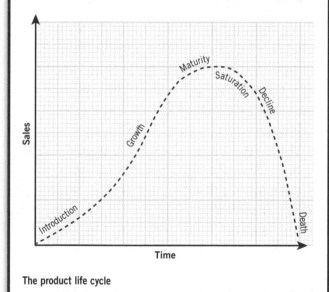

The product life cycle

Extending the Life Cycle

A business can extend the product life cycle through extension strategies, such as changes in advertising, packaging, renaming or re-branding, or improving the product.

The power of branding is important here, and having a strong brand image is important. Some of the most successful businesses are those that have a range of products, but all under a strong brand (for example, Adidas or Virgin).

Branding provides a clear identity across a range of products, supporting sales

✓ Maximise Your Marks

- You should be able to explain how the life cycle and Boston Matrix may be used as tools by a business. A* students will be able to link the product life cycle and the Boston Matrix by showing how each can be used to help a business decide whether to support a product – with advertising, for instance – or to let it decline and die.
- You should be able to balance arguments and give reasons why a particular business should or should not expand its product range. Bring in the other parts of the marketing mix to support your answer. Remember that supporting a product has implications for cash flow!

? Test Yourself

1. Describe what is meant by the marketing mix.
2. What is a product portfolio?
3. What problems might a wider product range bring to a business?
4. What happens at the 'maturity' stage of the product life cycle?

★ Stretch Yourself

1. What is a 'star' in the Boston Matrix?
2. Explain what managers are likely to do with each type of product on the Boston Matrix.
3. What strategies can a business use to extend the life cycle of a product?

The Marketing Mix: Price

How Businesses Use Price

Businesses use **price** to attract customers. As price falls, **more** is demanded; as it rises, **less** is demanded. Sometimes the amount that people buy is very **sensitive** to price. An example could be a luxury holiday that, with even a small price rise, becomes too expensive.

Sometimes the amount people will buy is not at all sensitive to price changes. Many necessities (such as bread and milk) come into this category.

Customers often use price levels as a signal of the **quality** of a product, often thinking that a higher price must mean better quality and a lower price worse quality. However, this is not always true.

Cost Plus Pricing

The most common way to set a price is probably **cost plus pricing**. This is where the business adds up the various costs of the product and then adds on a percentage for profit (called a **mark-up**).

So, for example, if a product cost £10 to make, £5 to transport to the shop and £1 in packaging, the total cost would be 10 + 5 + 1 = £16. A business that wanted a 10 per cent profit (called a profit margin) would then add on £1.60 (£16 ÷ 10) to make a price of £17.60.

This is not always as easy as it sounds, as it is often hard to decide the exact level of costs for a single product. Unless a business can work out exactly how much each product cost to make, transport, package, advertise, etc, accurate cost plus pricing can be very difficult.

distribution
profit
admin
labour
raw materials

Factors in cost-based pricing

Competitive Pricing

Where cost prices are difficult to calculate, a business is more likely to use a **competitive pricing** strategy.

Some competitive pricing is done by seeing what competitors are charging and matching this price. Other, special, types of price setting may be used by bigger businesses. Smaller businesses may not be able to use these. Examples are:

- **skimming** – a high price which people who want to be the first to own a new product will pay
- **penetration pricing** – a low price is set to gain market share
- **loss leaders** – a low price that does not cover costs is set to attract customers who then buy other, profitable, products
- **promotional pricing** – low prices set to boost sales in the short term; these are 'sale' prices.

Many of these pricing strategies can only be used where a business has a dominant position in a market. To use skimming, for example, a business must have a new product to bring to the market.

✓ Maximise Your Marks

Remember, when answering questions about marketing, that price is just one part of the mix and must be balanced with the other three areas. It is always the balance that is important.

Price and Markets

Businesses can use different types of price setting to compete. For example, they can try to increase growth and market share through skimming and penetration pricing.

Price techniques are only effective if used in the right type of market. For instance, in a market with a lot of competitors and very similar products, prices are also likely to be similar, so businesses will compete by adding value in other ways, such as better customer service.

Also, in any type of market, businesses must always set prices to attract customers.

The Right Strategy

Any type of pricing strategy that a business adopts must be suitable for both the product and the market in which the business is operating.

A burger bar, for example, could not use skimming, as this strategy is only effective for new technology products.

Businesses with a larger share of the market can often control price, while smaller businesses must accept market price.

❓ Test Yourself

1. Name a type of product that is sensitive to price changes, and one that is not.
2. Describe how a business would set a 'cost plus' price.
3. Explain why it is difficult to set an accurate 'cost plus' price.
4. Outline three pricing strategies a business can use to compete.

⭐ Stretch Yourself

1. Outline three types of low competitive pricing, with examples of where they might be used.
2. In what circumstances might skimming be a good strategy to use?
3. Explain, with an example, why not all price strategies can be used by all businesses.

The Marketing Mix: Promotion

Promotion

Promotion is the part of the marketing mix that is used to tell customers that products are available to buy and to persuade them to buy these products.

Promotion must be balanced against the other three areas of the marketing mix. It is no use, for example, promoting a product so well that the business cannot produce enough to meet demand, or expecting a product to sell without any promotion at all just because it is new.

Promotion can be expensive, so it has to be targeted carefully. Businesses also have to decide on the right mix of promotion types for their product and market.

Types of Promotion

Promotion is usually divided into two types. These are directly paid for advertising, called '**above-the-line**' expenditure and sales promotion, called '**below-the-line**' expenditure.

Advertising uses **media** such as print, television and radio. Media is the name used for the way the message is sent to customers.

Sales promotion includes cut-price offers, money-off coupons and 'specials', such as Buy One Get One Free (**BOGOF**).

Other types of promotion include competitions, free samples, **joint promotions** with other businesses and **public relations** (such as getting 'news' articles in papers). **Sponsorship** is where a business supports an event, a competition or a sports team which carries the name of the business.

Not all kinds of promotion result in increased profits. For example, an increase in sales, brought about by lowering prices or spending on advertising, might possibly increase profits but also might reduce them, depending on what the promotion has cost.

The wrong type of promotion can be catastrophic for a business. It is important to consider such factors as the costs of the promotion, who it might reach and what sort of service the market wants from the business.

Businesses can hand out leaflets to promote products

✓ Maximise Your Marks

- You should be able to balance the costs of promotion against its likely benefits and to discuss how spending a lot on promotions is not always an effective way to increase sales.
- Remember that promotion has to be appropriate. Think about why, for example, a BOGOF promotion on a daily newspaper would be less effective than one on a jar of coffee.
- A* students need to be able to recognise a marketing mix with too much emphasis on one or more of its parts. Each part of the marketing mix must be balanced with the others. Promotion is only effective if it is at the right level and to the right target market.

Promotion and Smaller Businesses

In promoting a product, a small business may have access to materials provided by the makers of the product.

These can include point-of-sale material, leaflets and other information. Small businesses can also inform customers through business cards and flyers.

They can also sponsor local events or teams and might, for example, provide shirts for a local football team, carrying its name.

While small businesses can use 'money off' and other sales promotions, they have to watch costs carefully. Many small businesses rely on their reputation and on 'word of mouth' recommendation, as this is both effective and free.

✓ Maximise Your Marks

Be sure that you know which types of promotion are right and affordable for a small business. Look at the business you are given in the examination and case study, and think about its size and market before suggesting a type of promotion.

Promotion and Larger Businesses

Larger businesses can access more promotional strategies. As they grow, they need to reach wider markets. They are also likely to be in a position to afford the more expensive types of promotion – methods that are not suitable for smaller businesses, such as national television or billboard campaigns and the sponsorship of famous teams or national events.

They can also often afford sales promotions, loss leaders and special offers that give better value to customers.

Although growing businesses can afford to use national advertising such as television, this is a lot more expensive, so they must be careful that spending is effective.

✓ Maximise Your Marks

Remember that even for large businesses, nationwide promotions are not always the most effective. It all depends on the type of product. For example, promoting superfast broadband in areas that cannot receive it is likely to upset customers and spoil the reputation of the business.

? Test Yourself

1. Describe the two functions carried out by promotion.
2. Outline above-the-line strategies suitable for a smaller business.
3. Name a below-the-line strategy suitable for a smaller business.
4. Outline two free promotional strategies used by smaller businesses.
5. Suggest strategies that would be suitable for a larger business but not a smaller one.

★ Stretch Yourself

1. Explain why an increase in sales as a result of a promotion may not always increase profits.
2. What factors need to be considered to avoid using the wrong type of promotion?

The Marketing Mix: Place

Marketing and Customers

Place

Place is that part of the marketing mix that refers to where a product is sold ('location') and to how the product gets there ('channels of distribution'). This includes any 'place' from where a customer can buy a good or service – not just shops, but also direct sales such as the Internet, catalogue sales or newspaper and magazine advertisements.

A business needs to choose the right place and distribution channels. This depends on the type of product and on the target market. Place must be balanced against the other three areas of the marketing mix. It is no use having a good, well-promoted product if customers cannot find it in the shops or obtain it any other way.

Distribution and Outlets

Distribution is the way that products are delivered to customers. Sometimes products are delivered directly to customers. This is called direct delivery, and it is in response to Internet or telephone orders, or to catalogue or direct mail sales.

Products are also delivered to sales outlets where customers can go to buy them. Different sales outlets will be used for different products and

markets. Retail outlets range from small corner shops to supermarkets, department stores and specialist stores. Delivery may also be to wholesalers. These can hold bulk stock, breaking it into smaller amounts for retailers.

Distribution channels may be short chain (direct to the customer) or long chain (many stages between producer and consumer).

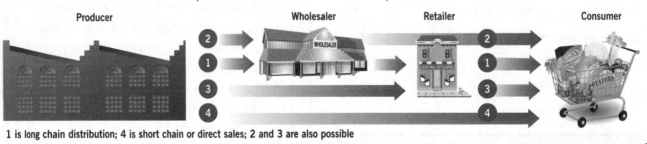

1 is long chain distribution; 4 is short chain or direct sales; 2 and 3 are also possible

Place and Growing Businesses

A growing business is likely to need to reach a wider customer base, so it may need more, or better, distribution channels.

Many producers sell to wholesalers or retailers, but might also be able to sell directly to customers. This depends on the type of product, type of market and costs of delivery.

Larger businesses can often use more efficient distribution channels and may even set up their own systems. For example, large supermarkets save money by having their own distribution and delivery networks.

✓ Maximise Your Marks

- Place and distribution are very important to the marketing mix. Imagine you are looking to buy a heavily promoted product but you find that it is not available because the business has run out. How would that make you, as a customer, feel?
- Better candidates will be able to suggest a marketing mix that is properly balanced for the product and its target market.

E-commerce

E-commerce is the name given to buying and selling goods and services via the Internet. With Internet sales, products are usually delivered directly to buyers. The product range can be easily viewed via a website and the business does not need expensive display or storage facilities.

E-commerce has opened up much wider markets, so that some products (such as music tracks and even movies) can now be more easily distributed online than in physical form. Even smaller businesses can take advantage of Internet sales, so long as they can afford the costs of delivery.

E-commerce has the advantage of convenience

Priorities

Businesses and customers have different priorities for 'place'. The business will be concerned with cost, the market and profit. Customers are more concerned with convenience, cost and reliability. These differing priorities must be balanced against one another.

Any business that considers setting up its own distribution channel must think it through very carefully. What are the benefits in terms of cost, reliability, control of supply? What might be the drawbacks?

Other considerations include whether the product is valuable, perishable, bulky, heavy or delicate – or, for example, whether the customer will need to try the product out.

Cost of delivery is also important. For example, although there are now many products available via the Internet, it is still most efficient to sell items online that have no delivery charges, such as downloads or services such as flights, train fares and holidays.

A company that gets these priorities wrong risks setting up a distribution channel that no one will want to use.

✓ Maximise Your Marks

Make sure that the products mentioned in your examination or case study can be sold and delivered via the Internet before suggesting this as a method of distribution. Sometimes the Internet is better employed as a way to promote a product rather than to deliver it.

❓ Test Yourself

1 Describe the two meanings of 'place' in the marketing mix.

2 Explain why different products use different distribution channels.

3 What are the main types of retail outlet?

4 What is meant by e-commerce?

5 Why has this become so important?

⭐ Stretch Yourself

1 Explain why a business is likely to have different priorities to the customer when it comes to distribution.

2 Explain which products are best suited to Internet sales, and why.

Customer Service

Why Customer Service Is Important

Success in business is not just about sales; it is about attracting customers and then keeping them. It is much more efficient to keep – or **retain** – customers than constantly having to attract new ones. Good customer service is vital to a business retaining customers.

Businesses therefore need to know what their customers want (which they find out through **market research**) and then provide it.

Businesses must give customers the right level of service – in other words, the level of service that matches customer expectations. Customers who are happy will return and become **repeat customers**. Good customer service helps to build **customer loyalty**.

Customers who are happy with purchases come back again!

Knowing the Customer

To provide the right level of service, a business needs to know what its customers want. If it has the right information about its market and competitors as well as its customers, it can then predict what customers want and provide it. The most powerful information comes from **direct customer contact** and listening to **customer feedback**.

Businesses need not only to listen to direct customer feedback, but to act on it. One unresolved complaint, for instance, is likely to do a lot of damage to a business's **reputation** and sales. Praise or positive feedback will encourage other customers.

Reliability is a central part of customer service. Businesses should fill orders accurately, deliver on time and both listen to and act on any complaints. They should be open as stated, hold stock to meet demand and sell products that perform to the standards customers expect.

💡 Boost Your Memory

Be careful to remember that there is a difference between 'customer' and 'consumer'. The customer buys the product but may be buying for someone else. The customer has to be happy at the point of purchase. The consumer has to be happy with the product.

✓ Maximise Your Marks

- Remember that businesses find out what customers want, and what competitors are doing, by using market research techniques.
- You should be able to talk about concepts like 'lifetime spend'. This is the amount of money a customer may spend at a business in his or her lifetime, and it shows why retaining customers is so important.

Types of Customer Service

There are four main areas of customer service:

- **Information** given directly to customers such as in a shop or via a call centre. It can also be on published material such as websites, packaging, catalogues and leaflets. Information must be accurate and true.
- Staff should be trained to give correct and accurate **advice**. In a specialist shop, customers are entitled to expect specialist advice.
- **After-sales service** refers to areas like delivery, packaging, guarantees, complaints, refunds and exchanges.
- Providing **convenience**, such as a good location or different ways to pay. Examples are card payments, hire purchase and credit deals.

Customer Loyalty Cards

Businesses can collect customer preferences by traditional means, such as asking them, but using electronic means is often more efficient.

One way to collect information is through **customer loyalty cards**. These are issued to customers to help retain them – by offering 'points' or offers or even **Airmiles**. The business uses them to keep a database of customers and to track their changing preferences. Whenever a card is swiped, the information on what is bought and how much has been spent is sent to update the database. The business can then change its marketing mix to suit customer wants.

Generally, only big businesses can afford to use customer loyalty cards, and this may give them a big advantage over smaller businesses. However, small businesses may be able to compete by providing better service because they know their customers better as individuals.

Customer Service and Targets

Customer service is often linked with business targets. After-sales service may be as important as the product. For example, a customer who bought an MP3 player but found that it would not play music would expect the business to replace or repair it. Businesses aim for and try to measure customer satisfaction so that they can set targets to reach – for example, responding to a complaint within a certain time, or answering the phone in so many rings.

✓ Maximise Your Marks

You should keep your eye on how customer service changes to keep up with technology. For example, most retailers now accept credit and debit cards, especially 'chip and pin' ones, but most nowadays refuse cheques.

❓ Test Yourself

1. Describe what is meant by 'the right level' of customer service.
2. What are the benefits to the business of good customer service?
3. Outline the four types of customer service.
4. What are customer loyalty cards?

⭐ Stretch Yourself

1. Explain how a business can show reliability to its customers.
2. How can a business link customer service and customer satisfaction to its targets?
3. In what sense can after-sales service be as important as the product?

Consumer Protection

Why Consumer Protection Is Needed

Not all businesses are always **fair** to their customers. Sometimes a business may try to **cheat** a customer. The Government has put laws in place to protect the consumer against such businesses.

To be fair to customers, businesses should only sell products that are as described, fit for purpose and not faulty or dangerous. Businesses have to make sure that the products they offer for sale do not break any of the **consumer protection laws**.

Some of the laws protect the consumer from harm; for instance, food must be fit for consumption. Others protect against cheating, such as giving false information about a product or incorrect pricing. There is an obligation on businesses to be fair and open. This includes being clear about **charges** and **penalties** and using accurate **weights and measures**.

Laws sometimes need to be changed to cover new business practices – Internet selling, for example. There are also now laws to cover consumer credit and its costs, including interest. These also set a **cooling-off period** for credit taken out away from a business (e.g. in a home).

Caveat Emptor

Businesses should treat customers fairly, but it is also up to the customers to check the quality and purpose of a product for themselves.

Customers must be careful that what they have bought is the right product for the purpose they need. They should make sure they read, understand and follow any instructions or restrictions. Buyers must check these for themselves. The Latin tag for this is '*caveat emptor*', which means 'let the buyer beware'.

The Main UK Acts

Britain's consumer protection is based on two main laws:

- **The Sale of Goods and Supply of Services Act** says goods must be of a satisfactory quality and meet the purpose for which they are sold. It also says when customers may have replacements or refunds and gives the right, in the case of a service not being properly carried out, for customers to have a refund or a replacement service charged to the original business.

- **The Trade Descriptions Act** prevents businesses from misleading their customers by describing products incorrectly. Products must be as described, of satisfactory quality and fit for purpose, as given by the business.

Parliament passes laws to protect the consumer

✔ Maximise Your Marks

You need to be able to explain the general ideas behind these laws, which are based on dealing with customers fairly.

European Union (EU) Laws

The **EU Unfair Commercial Practices Directive** has been introduced and underpins all UK consumer protection legislation. It brings in a general rule that no business should treat customers unfairly.

It has replaced some UK laws because it is wider ranging. It covers areas such as **high-pressure sales** and it also protects people who might be easily misled, such as old age pensioners or vulnerable people in their homes.

It covers all business sectors and activities, unlike the UK Act, which, for example, did not cover land and buildings.

The EU also passes directives, which the UK must follow

Consumer Responsibility

The law exists to protect consumers, but consumers themselves also have a responsibility. A key part of the law is that the consumer should check what they have bought, and that it does what they want it to do – in other words, that it is of **satisfactory quality**.

Satisfactory quality is linked to the product itself. Any product that does what it is meant to do (e.g. a match that strikes, or umbrella that keeps off the rain) is of satisfactory quality.

❓ Test Yourself

1. What is meant by consumer protection?
2. Outline the areas where consumers receive protection.
3. Explain two ways in which businesses must be fair and open.
4. Name the two main laws on which UK consumer protection is based.
5. Explain why the EU Directive is stronger than UK law.

⭐ Stretch Yourself

1. Describe what is meant by '*caveat emptor*' and explain why it is important.
2. Explain what is meant by 'satisfactory quality'.

Practice Questions

 Complete these exam-style questions to test your understanding. Check your answers on page 92. You may wish to answer these questions on a separate piece of paper.

Knowledge Questions

Answer questions 1–10 first, then read the case study before answering the other questions. Each knowledge question is worth 1 mark. For these questions, put a ring around the letter of the correct answer.

1 Which of the following is *not* a main source for desk research?

a) books **b)** newspapers and journals **c)** questionnaires **d)** the Internet.

2 One feature of field research is that it:

a) is cheap **b)** is up to date **c)** has been published before **d)** is easy to obtain.

3 The Boston Matrix can *not* be used by a business to see:

a) how a market is changing **b)** how a product is performing

c) how the product life cycle is developing **d)** what a competitor is doing.

4 Which of the following is *not* part of a product life cycle?

a) development **b)** maturity **c)** decline **d)** popularity.

5 Cost plus pricing is usually worked out by:

a) fixed cost plus variable cost **b)** cost plus mark-up **c)** start-up cost plus variable cost

d) revenue minus costs.

6 The traditional channel of distribution involving manufacturers, wholesalers and retailers is called:

a) short chain **b)** long chain **c)** intermediate chain **d)** no chain.

7 Above-the-line advertising expenditure is which of the following?

a) paid-for advertising **b)** sponsorship **c)** free advertising **d)** promotional pricing.

8 All of the following are included in customer service except:

a) providing information **b)** giving advice **c)** after-sales service **d)** promotional prices.

9 *Caveat emptor* is a Latin tag that means:

a) let the buyer beware **b)** let the seller be careful **c)** the price is right **d)** look out below.

10 The 'Kitemark' is the mark of quality used by:

a) Basic Standards Institute **b)** British Standards Institute **c)** British Services Incorporated

d) Basic Standards Institution.

Case Study

Jurgen thinks that there is a gap in the market for his new product. He has invented an additive that, when added to petrol, increases the miles per gallon by up to 30 per cent. The product has been tested in several chemical laboratories and proven to work, and it can be manufactured at a fairly low cost.

Jurgen has conducted a series of interviews with drivers, who have all shown enthusiasm. However, Jurgen does not yet have a national distributor for the product. The product is called ADD+.

Application Questions

11 Describe the market research information that Jurgen has collected and suggest possible drawbacks. (5)

....

....

12 Explain how Jurgen could undertake further market research. (5)

....

....

13 Explain where ADD+ is in the product life cycle and what this means to the business. (4)

....

....

Analysis and Evaluation Questions

14 Advise Jurgen of an appropriate marketing mix for his product. (8)

....

....

....

....

....

15 Advise Jurgen whether he should launch nationally or locally. (6)

....

....

....

16 Justify appropriate promotions for either a local launch or national launch of ADD+. (12)

....

....

....

....

....

....

....

How well did you do?

| 0–12 | Try again | 13–25 | Getting there | 26–38 | Good work | 39–50 | Excellent! |

Managing Staff

Recruitment

All businesses, even sole traders, may need to recruit staff. **Recruitment** is the process by which a business finds new staff. It starts with an advertisement describing the job. People apply with their **curriculum vitae** or **CV** (listing their work history, qualifications, etc.) and letters. The process of **selection** then begins. **Applicants** are shortlisted and invited to an **interview**. This can involve tests as well as questions. The best candidate is then offered the job.

The qualities that employers look for in candidates include qualifications, skills, experience, enthusiasm and attitude. Employees have the right to fair treatment. In all matters of employment, **discrimination** on grounds of gender, race, religion, creed, sexual orientation, disability or age is illegal. This includes the right to **equal pay** for equal work or responsibility.

Management of Change

The **management of change** can have a link to motivation, as changes to businesses will always affect the workforce. The changes may be made because the business needs to compete more effectively.

Workforces can be changed permanently by employing more (or fewer) people, or temporarily by using contract workers or part-time workers. If the change is managed well, there will be increased efficiency. Badly managed change can lead to problems.

⚈ Boost Your Memory

If you can't remember what types of motivation businesses use, think about what rewards would make *you* work harder!

Motivation

Businesses benefit from motivated staff. **Motivation** means people working more effectively because they want to, sometimes linked to a reward.

Businesses use many ways to motivate staff. Small businesses may offer motivation linked to their market. A shop could offer a reward for sales, for example. Some rewards are financial, such as bonuses or profit sharing; some are non-financial, such as praise and promotion, or supporting staff in training or education.

Businesses can try to keep employees motivated by keeping them happy. This could be by rewards (other than money), by making the job more interesting, or just by creating an environment in which people want to work.

The different **leadership styles** adopted by managers can also affect motivation. The best managers change their style to suit the situation.

Style	Means	Typical decision
Authoritarian or autocratic	Central, clearly defined orders	"Put it there."
Democratic	Staff take part in decision-making	"Let's take a vote on where to put it."
Laissez-faire	Staff make decisions within broad guidelines	"You decide where it goes."
Bureaucratic	Decisions are made according to the rules	"Rule 27a says it must go there."
Paternalistic	Managers consider workers' welfare when making a decision	"I think you'd be happier if it was there."

Motivation Theory

Of all the theories about motivation, the most quoted is **Maslow's Hierarchy of Needs**. Maslow says each worker meets a **need**, then aims for the **next higher level**. The needs he gives are:

1. survival or basic needs
2. security or safety
3. social needs
4. status or self-esteem
5. self-actualisation (or ambition reached).

For a business, these needs might be seen as a decent wage, job security and a pension, team working, a title or other symbol of status and an achievement of some final goal – perhaps a certain job within the business. Much motivation can be provided through praise and recognising good work.

Maslow's Hierarchy of Needs

✓ Maximise Your Marks

Maslow's Hierarchy is not the only important theory of motivation. You might find it useful also to look up and familiarise yourself with the theories of the American psychologist Frederick Herzberg.

Staff Retention

It is an expensive process to recruit, train and motivate staff, so it is better if a business can keep the workers it has, rather than have to appoint new ones all the time. **Staff retention** is therefore important for both efficiency and profitability.

A key way to retain staff is to value the work that they do. This may be part of management and motivation strategies, but could also be through promotion. **Staff development** refers to the improvements that workers carry with them – such as extra qualifications or more experience. Development and good conditions may help to retain workers. Flexible working practices are becoming more common. New technology allows people to work from home, meaning better use of their time, savings in travel and freedom to organise work as they wish.

✓ Maximise Your Marks

Not all examination boards are interested in motivation theory. Check with the specification for your own board that this is something on which you may be asked questions.

Remember, if you are asked how businesses can motivate workers, that changing the nature of their job can sometimes be a motivating strategy. Ideas include:

- **job rotation** – encouraging workers to move from one job to another at regular intervals
- **job enrichment** – giving the worker greater responsibility
- **job enlargement** – increasing the employee's responsibilities.

? Test Yourself

1. What is meant by recruitment?
2. Explain the stages in the recruitment process.
3. Give three ways in which it is illegal to discriminate.
4. What is the meaning of motivation?

★ Stretch Yourself

1. Why is the way that change is managed significant to workers?
2. Name two ways in which a business can encourage the retention of staff.

Methods of Payment

Remuneration

Workers have to be paid by a business for the work that they do. **Remuneration** is the term used to mean the way a worker is paid.
This may be a weekly or monthly **wage** or an annual **salary**:

- A wage is linked to the work done or time spent at work.
- A salary is an annual amount divided by 12 months. This payment is made monthly and is not linked to hours worked or tasks completed.

Workers must be certain that they will be paid, so that they can plan spending and saving. The UK government has set a **minimum wage**, which is the least amount per hour that any worker can legally be paid.

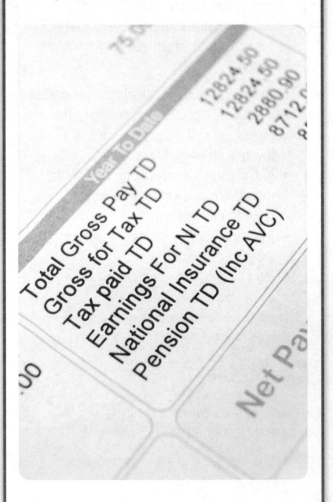

Payment Systems

There are a number of different ways to work out what a person should be paid. Each type of payment system has advantages and disadvantages to the worker and the business.

- **Piece rates** pay for the number of items made. This encourages speed but may lead to mistakes.
- **Time rates** are paid for the amount of time worked. Workers can sometimes earn overtime for extra time. Time rates can lead to slower work but fewer mistakes.
- **Commission** is a reward paid for increased sales. This encourages sales but may lead to customer dissatisfaction if too much pressure is used.

Managing Wage Costs

Businesses have to be careful to keep remuneration costs down while remaining efficient, by making decisions on cost, efficiency and availability of skills.

For example, they would have to decide when it would be better to employ a **temporary expert** in a particular field rather than have a permanent expert employee.

A temporary expert may be more expensive, but may be only needed for a short term. A permanent expert may only be needed now and again, but could bring other benefits such as knowledge of the business's systems or the ability to train others.

⚡ Boost Your Memory

- To help you remember the difference between wages and salaries, think of *Wages* as *Weekly* (both starting with the letter W).
- '*Pay The Cash*' should help you to remember Piece rates, Time rates and Commission as the three main ways to pay people.

Perks

There may be other benefits that come as part of a payment package. These are often called '**perks**'. Perks could include access to company pension schemes, provision of a company car, staff canteens, staff discounts, profit sharing and annual bonus payments.

Employees may also be entitled to **non-monetary benefits** that are linked to the market in which the business operates or the products that it sells. For example, a bank could offer cheaper loans or mortgages to its staff; a garage could offer free car servicing; or an airline could offer subsidised flights to employees.

Profit sharing encourages staff to work towards making the business a success by offering them a portion of the company's pre-tax profits, either as extra pay or as shares.

Perks are extra to normal pay but are nowadays quite important to people when it comes to choosing who they would rather work for. A good pension scheme, for example, is seen as vital.

✓ Maximise Your Marks

- Some examination boards need you to know about the various different ways to pay staff and how these can be used by a business to motivate workers and make them more efficient. Check whether or not your examination board will test you on this.
- You may be asked to work out payments from figures you are given, so you will need to remember about standard deductions from pay, such as income tax, National Insurance and pensions.

How Pay Is Used

Pay can be used as a way to motivate workers. This only works, however, after a certain basic level of pay and conditions has been met.

Pay may also be used to attract particular staff to ensure the business is flexible. For instance, it might employ part-time staff on lower wages to cover busy periods, or pay extra for freelancers or other outside specialists with special skills to bring to the business when needed.

Levels of pay will be set, firstly, according to qualifications, skill and experience. Further pay may be needed to retain staff or to gain particular skills.

? Test Yourself

1. What does 'remuneration' mean?
2. Explain the difference between a wage and a salary.
3. Give three examples of how workers are paid.
4. Explain how levels of pay are set.

★ Stretch Yourself

1. On what basis do businesses decide whether to use temporary or permanent staff?
2. Explain the advantages and disadvantages of temporary or permanent experts.
3. Give three possible perks that a business might offer.

Understanding Legislation

Rights of Employers and Employees

There are various laws to protect workers at work. These laws also explain the responsibilities that **employers** have to their **employees**.

Employees also have responsibilities to their employers. They should be on time, work to the best of their ability and do nothing to harm the business. In return, they have the right to decent and safe working conditions and fair pay for their work.

Basic **employment rights** therefore include the right to safe, healthy and reasonably comfortable working conditions, the right to protection from danger in the workplace, and the right to breaks and holidays.

Legal Rights

Some rights are basic human rights – for example, the right for an employee to be treated with courtesy and respect by an employer, and for the employer to treat the employee in the same way. Other rights are given through employment law.

Employees, by law, are entitled to a written statement giving rates of pay, terms and conditions of employment, pensions, notice periods and disciplinary procedures. They are entitled to:
- join a trade union
- be paid the minimum wage
- receive an itemised pay statement
- receive redundancy payments.

Employees must not be unfairly dismissed and they also have the right, under European laws, to take part in the management of the business for which they work.

When employment law is, or may have been, broken, **employment tribunals** sit to decide if either side has broken the law. They can award compensation to the business or the worker and even fine them for bad or illegal practices.

Equal Rights

The main laws on equality cover:
- Equal Pay (1970) – men and women should receive equal pay for equal work
- Sex Discrimination – (1975) men and women must get equal recruitment, training and promotion opportunities
- Race Relations – (1976) this made discrimination on the grounds of race or colour, marital status, nationality or ethnic group illegal. It set up the Race Relations Board to investigate complaints.
- Disability Discrimination – (1995) employers of 20 or more people cannot discriminate on grounds of disability.
- Age Discrimination – (2006) employers cannot exclude people from jobs because of age.

Health and Safety

Workers also have **health and safety** rights. The main law regarding health and safety is the 1974 **Health and Safety at Work Act** (HASAW).

The Act stipulates that both employers and employees have a general duty towards good health and safety practice in the workplace.

For example, employers must make sure that all workers have proper washroom and toilet facilities, ventilation, fire exits and levels of heating and lighting. Dangerous machines must be fitted with guards. Employees have a duty to take reasonable care for the health and safety of themselves and their fellow workers.

Industrial Relations

Industrial relations refers to the relationship between employer groups and employee groups, usually Trades Unions. Unions represent workers, fight for better conditions and act as pressure groups. Negotiations between groups is called **collective bargaining**.

A breakdown of industrial relations is called an **industrial dispute**. This can lead to industrial action. The main types of employee action are overtime bans, working to rule, go-slows and strikes.

Employers may, in certain cases, sack workers, or stage a 'lock out', refusing to allow them to work.

There are laws to try to stop industrial disputes. The main body that helps is the Advisory, Conciliation and Arbitration Service (ACAS).

💡 Boost Your Memory

Remember the letters in ACAS: it *Advises*, *Conciliates* (tries to bring agreement), *Arbitrates* (gives a ruling if there is no agreement) and is a *Service*.

Single Union Agreements

Disputes can be prevented through **single union agreements**, where all workers belong to the same Trade Union, allowing them to negotiate from a strong position. This also benefits employers, who only have to deal with one body.

Few disputes actually get as serious as strike action; they are usually resolved before this happens, due to the costs that a strike can incur to both employer and employees.

✓ Maximise Your Marks

It can help you in the exam to think about what you would expect from your workers if you were an employer – and what you would expect from an employer if you were the worker.

❓ Test Yourself

1. What are the main rights and responsibilities of employers?
2. Outline the main responsibilities of employees.
3. Give three ways in which workers must get equal treatment.
4. Explain what is meant by 'industrial relations'.

⭐ Stretch Yourself

1. List three things required under health and safety law.
2. How can a single union agreement prevent problems for employees and employers?
3. Explain why few disputes actually get as far as strike action.

Training and Performance Review

Training

Once appointed, new staff may need training. An **induction training** programme introduces them to the workplace and the job. It covers basic information such as how the business works, what the job entails and so on.

Further training benefits the business by improving efficiency. It is also of value to the employee in developing skills and knowledge.

Businesses can carry out training themselves or use external **agencies**. Big businesses are likely to have their own training departments. Agencies can be more effective at training, but tend to be expensive.

Some training may be **on the job training**, where the employee is trained while working. This may reduce the worker's effectiveness while it is taking place. Alternatively, **off the job training** could take place away from the workplace.

Development

Development is different from training. Training is providing the worker with skills and knowledge that fit in with those that the business needs. Development, on the other hand, provides better skills and knowledge for the worker him/herself.

Development can be seen as being of greater benefit to the worker than to the business, although, of course, a better trained or more skilful worker also brings benefits to the business. Development increases the skills and knowledge of the worker and may also lead to additional qualifications as it may involve, for example, taking professional examinations or undertaking further study.

Lifelong Learning

Many businesses expect employees to keep re-training and improving their skills in order to keep up with changes to jobs and the way they are carried out. Technology and jobs change so fast that different skills will be needed all the time.

This is called **lifelong learning** and is important to businesses so they have trained staff, and also to employees so that their skills are current.

A potential drawback for the business, though, is that better qualifications and skills make an employee more expensive and more flexible. So, although the employee will be of greater value to the business, they will probably have to be paid more if they are to stay rather than be tempted away by other employers.

✔ Maximise Your Marks

Remember that training is good for the business, making workers more efficient. Development is good for the worker, making them better qualified.

Appraisal and Performance Review

Appraisal is the process that allows an employee to exchange views with the employer, usually in a formal or semi-formal setting. A good appraisal may result in rewards or might lead to promotion.

Appraisal can help to identify where **progress** has been made and where the employee might need **support**. Many businesses also have performance management systems.

Performance management reviews are not as two-way as appraisals, tending to focus on the employer's view. They are often linked to **key performance indicators** (KPIs) that benefit the business more than the employee.

Appraisal and performance management systems are often built in to the organisation of a business as ways to increase efficiency.

Carrying out an appraisal

Striking a Balance

Training, development and appraisal are ways to show staff that they are valued, so they can help with motivation and with retaining staff.

There can be a conflict of interest, though, between training and development. A business may be keen to train a worker in its own methods and operations. This makes the worker more valuable to them.

On the other hand, if the business encourages worker development, this makes the worker better qualified and more attractive to other businesses. They may also want higher pay to go with their higher qualifications. Employer and employee must strike a balance so that both are happy.

❓ Test Yourself

1. What is meant by 'induction training'?
2. What benefits does development bring to the worker?
3. What is meant by 'appraisal'?
4. Why are performance management reviews more for the benefit of employers than employees?

⭐ Stretch Yourself

1. What is lifelong learning?
2. Why is lifelong learning important?
3. Explain the possible conflict of interest that arises when a business trains a worker.

Practice Questions

Complete these exam-style questions to test your understanding. Check your answers on page 93. You may wish to answer these questions on a separate piece of paper.

Knowledge Questions

Answer questions 1–10 first, then read the case study before answering the other questions. Each knowledge question is worth 1 mark.

In the following questions, fill in the spaces with the correct term.

1 .... means people working more effectively because they want to, sometimes linked to a reward.

2 It is an expensive process to recruit, train and motivate staff, so it is better if a business can keep its workers. This is called ....

3 .... is the term used to mean the way a worker is paid.

4 The .... is the least any worker can legally be paid.

5 .... is a reward paid for increased sales.

6 Basic .... means the rights to safe, healthy and reasonably comfortable working conditions in the workplace.

7 The main law regarding health and safety is the 1974 Health and Safety at Work Act, which is abbreviated to ....

8 .... introduces a new worker to the workplace and the job.

9 .... is the process that provides better skills and knowledge for the worker him or herself.

10 .... is the process that allows the employee to exchange views with the employer in a two way dialogue.

Case Study

21st Century Tech is a business that collects secure information for a banking and investment group. One of its main functions is to maintain the database of customer information, account details and passwords.

The person who looked after the database has recently been promoted within the company and a new database operative is needed. The person in this post would be paid a salary linked to his or her qualifications and would receive the perk of a free laptop. They would be able to work at home for at least part of the week.

As the database is updated only four times a year, the business is trying to decide whether to employ a temporary person to do the job or take on a permanent employee.

Application Questions

11 Describe the type of working if the employee can work at home sometimes. (3)

12 How might being given a free laptop motivate the person appointed? (2)

Analysis and Evaluation Questions

13 Do you think that 21st Century Tech should employ a permanent, full-time database expert, or just call in a temporary expert four times a year? Give reasons for your answer.

(10)

How well did you do?

| 0–6 | Try again | 7–12 | Getting there | 13–19 | Good work | 20–25 | Excellent! |

Methods of Production

Production

Businesses need to make products to sell. **Production** describes the ways that raw materials and other inputs are turned into the final product, called output.

Production combines **the factors of production** which are:
- land – somewhere to operate from
- labour – human effort
- capital – machinery and tools
- enterprise – the ability to put factors together.

Production can be seen as a process involving **inputs**, **transformation** and **outputs**, as follows:
- Inputs are the raw materials, components or part-finished goods plus labour, power, machinery, etc.
- Transformation is the process of manufacture, refining or processing that changes the inputs into:
- Outputs, which are the finished or part-finished goods.

Production Methods in Small Businesses

The main methods of production in small businesses are:
- **Job production** – where a product is a 'one-off' made to individual specifications, for example a made-to-measure suit. This is labour-intensive and expensive. Almost all services are job-produced.
- **Batch production** – where the same inputs are used to produce different batches or groups of output. It is used, for instance, if different sizes or colours are needed. For example, the same pair of shoes will be made in different

sizes. Batch production can be used for anything made in different sizes or colours. All clothes not job-produced will be made in batches, as well as all cars that are not custom-built. Many drugs and most confectionery products are batch-produced.

Services are produced to individual standards. For goods, some are produced individually, while others are produced in larger amounts and standard sizes or shapes.

Lean Production

Lean production is being more efficient by reducing the amount of inputs. The biggest cut is usually in terms of time. New computer technology can help businesses run '**Just-In-Time**' (JIT) systems.

In a JIT system, inputs such as parts arrive just as they are needed. There is no need for stock to be held, nor for inputs or outputs to be stored. However, if an input fails to arrive in time the production process is stopped.

Working under pressure could lead to mistakes, so staff need proper training to cope with JIT systems.

✔ Maximise Your Marks

JIT means that, providing inputs arrive, there is no break in production. However, if they fail to arrive on time, this can be a disaster. You need to weigh up the advantages and disadvantages to a business of such a break in production. If, for example, special materials have been prepared, or ingredients mixed, a break in production may be very expensive.

Production Methods in Larger Businesses

Larger businesses can use a third method of production, called **flow production**. Here a product is processed or built as it moves along a production line. Examples include car manufacture (assembly line) or oil refining (processing). Using flow production allows for **specialisation** and **automation**, with parts of the process carried out by robots.

Flow production allows **division of labour** to be used. Each worker can specialise on a particular task. This makes them more efficient. However, it may also **demotivate** them through boredom. The type of flow production where transformation involves a process (such as baking, refining, mixing), is sometimes called **process production**.

Production lines can be automated

Advantages and Disadvantages

There are advantages and disadvantages to specialisation and division of labour. Workers can be good and efficient at a certain task, but they can also become bored and lose interest.

Job rotation (moving between jobs) and **job enrichment** (making the job more interesting) can help. Boring and repetitive jobs can also be automated. This is good for the business's efficiency, but not for workers who need employment.

❓ Test Yourself

1. Describe the process of production.
2. What is 'job production'?
3. What is 'batch production'?
4. Explain what is meant by 'division of labour'.

⭐ Stretch Yourself

1. Explain what is meant by 'lean production'.
2. List some advantages and disadvantages of specialisation and division of labour.
3. Describe how workers' boredom could be relieved.

Operations

Business Expansion and Growth

Why Businesses Grow

Businesses range in size from sole traders with no employees to very large multinationals employing thousands. To get from one to the other needs **growth** – increasing the number of products for sale, the range of products, or **market share**.

Businesses change as markets change. Products may become **out of date** and are replaced with newer, better products. New competitors may enter the market.

Businesses can benefit from growth by becoming more efficient. They may also become the **dominant** business in a market, from where they may be able to control price or demand.

How Businesses Grow

A business can grow through either **internal** (called '**organic**') or **external** growth.

Internal means growth from within, at a gradual pace. Changes from internal growth tend to be slow and easily managed. External means joining with other businesses. This is called **integration** and may be:
- horizontal – businesses at the same stage of production
- vertical – to a previous stage of production (backward) or a further stage (forward)
- lateral – to a similar but not directly related market
- conglomerate – to an unrelated area (also called diversification).

When businesses agree to join, this is a **merger**.

If one bids to buy the other, this is a **take-over**.

Businesses can also grow by **franchising**.

Integration

The direction of integration depends on where the businesses sit in the **chain of production**.

A bakery is a good example, as shown in the diagram below. A bakery that:
- buys another bakery = horizontal integration
- buys a flour supplier = backward vertical
- buys a sandwich shop = forward vertical
- buys a confectioner = lateral
- buys a bicycle maker = conglomerate.

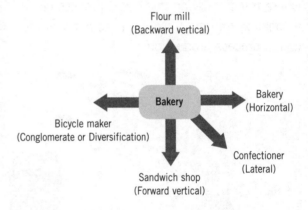

Businesses and consumers can gain or lose from integration.

Integration could mean that a business takes its competitors out of the market. This could mean that it could then reduce consumer choice, charge higher prices and make more profit. This could be a disadvantage for consumers, so national bodies (like the Office of Fair Trade) are often set up to make sure that the bigger business is not going to disadvantage customers.

✓ Maximise Your Marks

The **management of change** is an important factor to remember when talking about how a business has coped with changes in the market, and with its own growth. Remember that there can also be disadvantages to growth – like managers becoming more remote from workers.

Economies and Diseconomies of Scale

Businesses that grow can gain from **economies of scale**. Those within the control of the business are internal, such as:

- financial – lenders give better rates to bigger businesses
- bulk buying – buying at lower prices
- technical – specialist machines and workers
- risk bearing – risk spread over more products and markets
- marketing.

There are also **diseconomies of scale**, such as longer chains of communication, more remote management and more complex production processes.

External economies are from growth of the industry. This means bigger markets and more availability of skilled labour. It also leads to the growth of smaller, specialised businesses providing services to the industry.

Financing Growth

A business must find money to pay for growth, and larger businesses have access to more sources of finance. They will have more assets and more profit than small businesses. Internal sources include **retained profits** and the sale of unwanted assets. Retained profit is an important source, as interest does not have to be paid, nor money paid back to a lender.

External sources include loans and share issues. A private limited company might go public and raise money through shares. A plc can also raise money by selling more shares.

✓ Maximise Your Marks

- Remember that only bigger businesses can benefit from economies of scale, so think about the sources of finance that are available to bigger, rather than smaller, businesses. These include share issues and selling off unwanted assets, as well as profit.
- Sometimes you will be asked to make recommendations. Would it be wise, for example, for the business you have been given to merge with another and, if so, in what direction? Remember, there is not always a right answer but you must justify any decision that you make.

❓ Test Yourself

1. Give three ways in which a business's growth can be measured.
2. Explain what is meant by 'internal growth'.
3. What is meant by 'external growth'?
4. Give three methods of integration and explain what the terms mean.
5. List the four main economies of scale.

★ Stretch Yourself

1. Explain the advantages and disadvantages of integration to consumers and businesses.
2. Give two internal and two external ways of financing growth.

Managing and Maintaining Quality

Operations

Quality

Quality goods or services are ones that do what they are supposed to do. In UK law, this means that they are **fit for purpose**. If a product does not do what it should, then the consumer has the right to demand his or her money back.

Growing businesses may face quality problems as production expands. All production that is not up to quality standards is wasted and therefore causes increased costs. A growing business may find that it is producing more of a product, or different products as it moves into new markets. In either case, it must be careful to maintain the quality of its product by ensuring that both inputs and processes are quality controlled.

This can be through traditional **quality control** or **quality assurance**. Traditional quality control systems check quality at the end of production. This means that any faulty production is lost production, and inputs go to waste. External inspectors can be used to check quality, but this can be very expensive. The business must weigh up this cost against possible lost sales from not maintaining quality.

In quality assurance systems, it becomes everyone's responsibility to maintain quality at every stage of production.

A business will usually set its own quality systems to make sure that production standards are even better than the consumer expects.

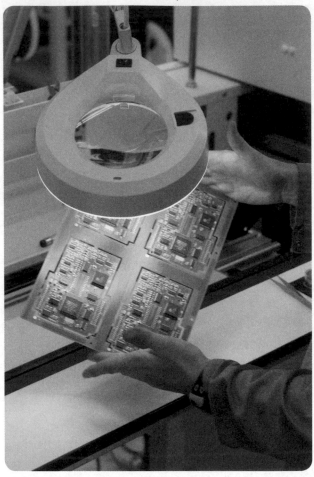

Quality control checking

Quality Versus Cost

Quality comes at a cost, but lack of quality could mean an even greater cost! Managers must keep a constant watch to ensure that production is cost-effective. This means keeping costs down to allow prices to remain competitive. However, costs should not be cut at the expense of quality. Although there are costs to maintaining quality, there can be higher costs in terms of reputation and falling demand if quality is not maintained.

Businesses need to look at the minimum that the law requires and then add to this in order to compete and to gain customers. However, there has to be a balance struck between the cost of any improvement and savings made or possible increases in sales.

✓ Maximise Your Marks

When discussing quality, it is important to stress that it means 'fit for purpose' – anything that 'does what it says on the tin' is a quality product.

58

Quality Standards

There are international standards of quality that businesses can earn. These show other businesses (and their customers) that this business is keen to maintain quality. One of the most important is **ISO 9001**, an international standard that has to be renewed each year.

In the UK, the Kitemark symbol is used to show that products have passed quality tests set by the **British Standards Institute** (BSI).

There are other standards for quality management, customer service, etc. For example:

- the **Customer Service Excellence Standard** (replaced the **Charter Mark** in 2008)
- the **European Foundation for Quality Management** promotes the EFQM Excellence model for management
- **IIP** is **Investors in People**, for quality human resources policies.

✔ Maximise Your Marks

- Don't confuse 'quality' with 'expensive' or 'cheap'. It has nothing to do with the price of goods or services. A quality product is just one that does as it should. A match that strikes first time is as much a quality product as an expensive diamond ring.
- Quality systems and ideas are changing all the time, so make sure that you are up to date – for example, as mentioned above, old standards like the Charter Mark become replaced by newer, more up to date standards. Better candidates will know this.

Japanese Ideas

TQM and *Kaizen* were both developed in Japan.

TQM stands for **Total Quality Management**. The idea is that every person involved in production is responsible for quality. Each worker (and each machine) checks for quality as the product enters an area, as it is processed and before it leaves. 'Total' also extends to parts, materials and other inputs. A truly TQM business will only deal with other TQM businesses.

Kaizen means 'continuous improvement' and states that everyone should see how their process could be made better (however small the change). In this way, many small changes can lead to big improvements in quality.

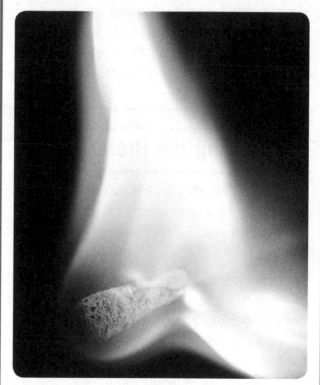

A match that strikes is a quality product – it does its job

❓ Test Yourself

1. What is meant by 'quality' goods or services?
2. Describe traditional quality control.
3. Describe Total Quality Management.
4. What is meant by '*Kaizen*'?

★ Stretch Yourself

1. Explain the balance that managers must maintain between cost and quality.
2. Name three important quality standards.

Research and Good Design

Why Good Design Is Important

One way in which a business can establish a **USP (Unique Selling Point)** is to make its products **stand out** from others. Businesses have a much better chance of being a success if their products have unique features or properties.

One way to achieve this is through good **design**. A good design can be used like branding to differentiate one product from another.

Good design does not mean that something is modern, or fashionable – it just means that the product does what the customer wants it to do. This is the definition, in business, of a 'quality' product.

Elements of Good Design

Designers design products to fit in with the reasons why customers want to buy them. Customers may want a product to work effectively, they may want it to look good or fashionable, or modern, or they may just want to be able to buy it at a particular price.

The designer has to balance these various elements when designing new or improved goods and services. He or she will look at how the product will do its job (known as its '**function**'), how it will look (known as its '**aesthetic**') and how it can be made and sold at a competitive price.

Promoting the Brand

Businesses can trade on the idea of 'quality' through advertising or promotions that show the product in a good light, or make certain claims for it.

Good design can often be embedded in the idea of a brand. If people come to think of a particular branded product as having good design features, then the reputation of the brand can be extended to other goods to support the business. Apple, for instance, built up a reputation for attractive and innovative design, and as a result, all of its products are seen as 'cool'.

Many cosmetic and bathroom products for both women and men have very large promotional budgets, and are part of branded ranges, but may not actually be any more effective than much cheaper products. The reason for buying them is fashion (a brand name) and a *belief* in the function advertised.

✓ Maximise Your Marks

- Think about why you are buying a product whenever you go shopping. Is it just because it does a job (food, to stop you being hungry) or because of other features (branded food, because it is 'better'). Do you mostly buy for function or aesthetic? Considering these factors may help if asked about the importance of good design in the exam.
- If you are asked to compare one product with another, think about not just its functional features but also its aesthetic ones. You need to judge which of those features is most attractive to the buyer, making it most likely to be promoted.

Combining Design Elements

For some businesses, function is most important – a new drug must work rather than look good. In other businesses, such as fashion, function may take second place to how something looks. A pair of shoes may be fashionable but may be hard to walk in, or cause damage to feet.

The best products have all three elements. A jacket may have a function (to keep the buyer warm and dry), be fashionable (perhaps with a designer label) and also be at the right price.

Sometimes one aspect wins out over another. Someone may buy a jacket because it is fashionable rather than because it will keep them warm.

Research and Development

Research and Development, or **R&D**, takes place in departments of larger businesses or, in some cases, is what the business does. Scientific research will look at new products, new processes and new ways of combining materials. R&D tries to develop products that have the balance that will attract the customer to buy based on the design mix of function, aesthetic and cost.

Sometimes it is hard to strike a balance. Cutting costs by using cheaper inputs or materials could affect the way the product functions. Trying to improve the aesthetic appearance could increase costs and prices.

✓ Maximise Your Marks

- Remember, a good product must work properly, and look good. Can you think of products you have bought with all three design elements?
- Many new products are the result of R&D that has looked at what people want and then developed it. Many new technology products fall into this category. Think about how TVs have developed – stereo, surround sound, flat screen, HD, 3D. What could be next?

? Test Yourself

1. Explain how a business can establish a Unique Selling Point.
2. Explain the difference between 'function' and 'aesthetic' for a product.
3. Using an example of a product, discuss why function is more important.
4. Using an example of a product, discuss why aesthetic is more important.
5. Explain the balance that R&D is trying to achieve.

★ Stretch Yourself

1. Explain how a business can trade on the idea of 'quality'.
2. What is meant by embedding good design into the idea of a brand?

Operations

Managing Stock

Stock and Stock Control

Businesses that produce goods need raw materials or components. Even service businesses may hold **stock** of some sort; for example, a hairdresser needs a stock of products like shampoos and lotions.

Most businesses hold an amount of stock or **inventory**. This could be raw materials, partly finished goods, components or even finished goods waiting to be delivered.

Efficient **stock control** is important, because keeping down the costs of storing and moving stock can lower prices. Money spent on stock is **tied up**, so businesses try to keep stock at a minimum. The **inventory turnover rate** measures how fast stock is moving so helps to manage stock. It is measured as the cost of sales/average inventory investment. **FMCGs** (Fast Moving Consumer Goods) turn over the quickest.

Businesses need systems to keep track of stock in order to ensure that they have the right amount of stock for their immediate needs.

The amount of stock held will depend on the type of business. Certain types of stock will only be held in small amounts. If, for example, stock is highly valuable, or perishable, or it is expensive to store, the business may hold little of it. If stock is hard to buy (perhaps in short supply) or takes a long time to deliver, the business may be forced to hold high levels of it, regardless of the cost.

Chocolate bars and sweets are FMCGs

The Importance of Maintaining Stock Levels

Almost all businesses need stock of some sort, but it is most important to businesses that are producing goods, particularly if they are involved in complex production processes and production lines.

If stock is not available, the whole production process could halt and many inputs could be wasted, especially in businesses that are involved in processing.

For example, if, halfway through making a nutty chocolate bar, a vital input (like nuts) is missing, then the whole process is spoiled.

This is not just important for businesses that produce goods. Many service businesses also need products or parts in order to trade.

✓ Maximise Your Marks

If you are asked questions about stock, think about the sort of stock that a business could *not* hold. This includes stock that is really expensive, stock that may deteriorate (like food or ingredients for food processes) or stock that is difficult to store (that must be kept at a set temperature, perhaps).

Operations

Striking a Balance

There is a cost attached to holding stock, so managing the quantity held is important to keep costs down. It is important for a business to hold as little stock as possible, but still enough for its needs.

A business must strike a balance between holding too much stock and holding too little. Holding too much stock means costs that could be avoided.

Not holding enough could mean loss of production or sales.

Just-In-Time (**JIT**) stock control plans for stock to arrive just as it is needed, as opposed to holding stock '**Just-In-Case**'. Just-In-Time is cheaper and more efficient than Just-In-Case, but carries risks if stock fails to arrive.

Traditional Stock Control

The figure of a **bar gate stock chart** shows how a traditional stock control system works.

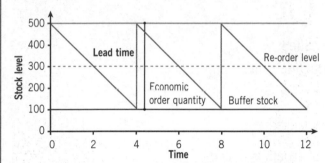

Maximum and **minimum** stock levels are set by the business. These represent the most and least stock that the business ever wishes to hold (or is capable of holding). Once stock falls below a certain level (the **re-order level**), more is ordered. This takes time to arrive (called '**lead time**') and is, ideally, delivered as stock reaches its minimum level.

As insurance, many businesses hold more than this level of stock so that there is a buffer against a shortfall or a delay. This is called **buffer stock**.

The **economic order quantity** (**EOQ**) is the amount of stock level to be ordered at one time for the purpose of keeping annual inventory costs to a minimum.

Operations

Practice Questions

 Complete these exam-style questions to test your understanding. Check your answers on page 94. You may wish to answer these questions on a separate piece of paper.

Knowledge Questions

Answer questions 1–10 first, then read the case study before answering the other questions. Each knowledge question is worth 1 mark. For these questions, put a ring around the letter of the correct answer.

1 A good or service that does what it is supposed to do is called a:

a) cheap product **b**) expensive product **c**) quality product **d**) assured product.

2 Traditional quality control systems check quality when?

a) during production **b**) at the start of production **c**) at the end of production

d) once the good is sold.

3 Producing large quantities on a production line is called:

a) job production **b**) flow production **c**) batch production **d**) lean production.

4 Division of labour allows which of the following?

a) job production **b**) delegation **c**) induction **d**) specialisation.

5 Efficient production, using the minimum number of inputs is called:

a) job production **b**) flow production **c**) batch production **d**) lean production.

6 The production method when parts etc. arrive only as they are needed is called:

a) test in time **b**) just in time **c**) batch production **d**) mean production.

7 'TQM' stands for

a) Total Quality Management **b**) Top Quality Management **c**) Total Quantity Management

d) Total Quality Matters.

8 Which of the following is not a part of good design?

a) aesthetic **b**) competitive price **c**) function **d**) brand.

9 A business is unlikely to hold a lot of stock unless it is:

a) valuable **b**) perishable **c**) cheap **d**) expensive to store.

10 The stock level graph is called a 'bar gate' graph as it resembles:

a) a field gate **b**) a bar graph **c**) a line graph **d**) an open gate.

Case Study

Kernels Ltd has been producing chocolates and other confectionery for over 100 years under the motto 'quality chocolates for quality people'. It is based in the Midlands town of Brunton, where it produces boxes of chocolates in several sizes. It is well known for its 'chocolate fountains' – large chocolate sculptures made to order for special occasions. Its main rival in many of its markets is Holborn plc. Holborn has been enjoying record profits over the last few years through expanding into overseas markets. Recently it has made an offer to buy Kernels, saying it could cut costs by no longer making chocolate fountains. It says it is offering a fair price for Kernels.

Application Questions

11 What is meant by a 'quality product'? (3)

12 Describe the types of production at Kernels. (6)

13 Explain what could happen to the business if cost-cutting means worse quality. (3)

Analysis and Evaluation Questions

14 Explain how consumers might gain or lose from the planned merger. (8)

15 Explain the type of integration proposed and its possible benefits. (6)

16 Looking at possible gains and losses from the merger, would you advise Kernels to accept or not? (12)

Operations

How well did you do?

| 0–12 | Try again | 13–24 | Getting there | 25–36 | Good work | 37–48 | Excellent! |

Obtaining Finance

Finance and Accounts

Why Businesses Need Finance

All businesses need finance:
- They need finance at start-up, to buy, for example, materials, to pay for power or fuel, to buy or rent equipment and premises.
- They need finance to pay wages and suppliers and to advertise that they are open for business.
- They need finance to grow and to compete.

For a small business, this money will come from its owners and their friends, or from lenders or people who are willing to take a risk and invest in the business. Small businesses will usually start with the **owner's funds** as finance.

Because small businesses might struggle, there are government and charitable organisations to help them. Business support is available from the Government through the **Business Start Up Scheme** and through charities like **The Prince's Youth Business Trust** (usually called **The Prince's Trust**).

Company Finance

Companies can access **internal** sources of finance, such as their own profit, or by selling off unwanted assets. If a business has an asset that it no longer needs or uses, it can sell it.

Such sales of equipment that is no longer needed might allow the business to buy new equipment or to modernise.

A private company could decide to access **external** sources of finance. It could 'float' on the stock exchange to raise finance, or, if already a plc, could issue more shares. Although this brings in more money, it also gives more shareholders control over the business.

Borrowing

Almost all businesses exist by **borrowing** finance. Sometimes this is at start-up, in order to buy, for example, initial stock or equipment. Or it could be later, to pay for stock, power and other inputs before production can be sold, or to finance growth.

Borrowing can be done either **formally** or **informally**.

Formal borrowing includes such arrangements as bank loans and mortgages.

Informal borrowing includes the spreading of payments. For example, power and energy payments can be made quarterly or monthly rather than in one lump sum.

✔ Maximise Your Marks

Remember that it is not difficult to float a company to raise finance, but it has to be reasonably big and have a secure future. Companies that do go public have to state what they want the money for to persuade people to invest.

Borrowing as Part of Operations

Many businesses finance through borrowing. The most common types are those that form part of the operation of a business. These are:

- **Trade credit** – when a business promises to pay a supplier later for goods received now. Hopefully the goods will be sold by the time the business has to pay the supplier.
- **Hire purchase** – the business pays a deposit and buys an asset over a set period of time in instalments.
- **Leasing** – the business term for renting machinery, vehicles and equipment.

All businesses can use any profits that they keep. This is called **retained profit**, because it has not been shared out (or distributed). Of course, profits that are used as finance for a business are not then available to keep shareholders happy. Shareholders may want a return on investment now, rather than waiting for the future.

Owners may also raise finance from friends and family or from private investors called **venture capitalists**.

Banks and Borrowing

Businesses may also borrow from banks and financial institutions through:

- **Overdrafts** – permission to take more out of an account than there is in it, up to an agreed limit. This is usually **flexible** and **interest** is only charged on what is actually owed.
- **Loans** – borrowing a fixed amount, for a fixed term, with regular repayments made and interest charged on the full amount for the **term** of the loan.
- **Mortgages** – long-term loans used to buy expensive items like land or buildings, secured on the item bought.

The Government encourages banks to lend and guarantees some small business loans. Businesses will usually need to provide the lender with a detailed **business plan**, saying how they intend to spend the money and how they intend to repay it.

✓ Maximise Your Marks

- Remember that every formal loan comes with a cost, usually in terms of interest on the loan, but sometimes in terms of extra control the lender takes over the operation of the business.
- Be careful when talking about venture capitalists. Although they are often in the news, they tend to back larger businesses rather than small start-ups. So, before using them as an example, check that they make sense in the context of the business you are describing.

❓ Test Yourself

1. Outline three reasons why businesses need finance.
2. What is the most usual finance for small sole traders?
3. Give two ways in which businesses might get financial support.
4. Give three types of borrowing that form part of the operation of a business.
5. Name the two types of borrowing that are central to businesses. Give examples.

★ Stretch Yourself

1. Give examples of internal sources of finance.
2. What are the three ways businesses can borrow from banks and financial institutions?

Revenues, Costs and Breakeven

Costs and Revenues

All businesses produce goods or services for sale:
- If they produce goods, then there are raw materials and other inputs like labour and power that cost money.
- Services also have costs, such as labour and marketing.

Costs are filed under various categories:
- **Fixed costs** (also called **overheads**) such as rent are **indirect costs** that do not vary with output and are paid regardless of production.
- **Variable costs**, such as parts, power and ingredients, vary directly with output. **Total cost** is **fixed cost** plus **variable cost**. Some variable costs vary with output, but not directly. These are **semi-variable** costs. Examples include the cost of overtime payments, or a shop opening for longer hours.
- **Set-up costs** (or **start-up** or 'sunk' costs) are paid once to set up the business.
- **Operating costs** (or **running costs**) are those that have to be continually paid. These may be fixed costs such as rent, or variable costs such as wages.

Revenue is the money made from sales. Revenue is measured as sales × price, but it may also come from other sources, such as **rent** or **interest**.

✓ Maximise Your Marks

- It is important to remember which costs are which, especially as some have several different names. For example, one business may call its fixed costs fixed, another may call them overheads and another may call them indirect costs.
- The nature of fixed and variable costs is to do with output, or the amount produced. Think of fixed costs as those that must be paid even if the business did not produce anything, for example basic power, telephone costs, rent and rates. They are fixed when the business sets up.

Breakeven

Breakeven is where total costs equal total revenue. At this point, the business is making neither a profit (when revenue is greater than costs) nor a loss. Changes in any cost, or in revenue from sales, will alter the breakeven point. Breakeven can be seen on a graph, or calculated through a formula. The formula can be used to work out the **contribution** of each sale towards breakeven. There are two parts to the formula:
- Price per unit – variable cost per unit = contribution to fixed costs.
- Fixed costs ÷ total contribution = breakeven level of sales.

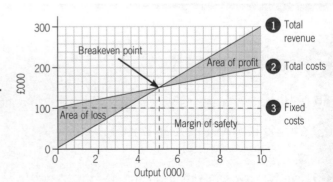

Using Breakeven

Breakeven can be used as a tool to predict the effect of changes in costs and revenues on forecast profit or loss. For example, it can be used for 'what if' scenarios to predict what would happen if factors like costs, revenues and sales changed.

Breakeven be used to predict where a profit will be made and it can help the business to plan. At the start of a venture, profit is not certain, and breakeven can help a business to 'guesstimate' where it might be.

The problem with breakeven is that it is difficult to say exactly where it is for a business, especially if there are many products being sold. It therefore can have limited use as it can be difficult to always say which costs are which, or which particular product, out of a range of products, is contributing.

Contribution calculations can show which products are making a profit, though, so these can be a useful tool. The contribution formula needs to be used to make breakeven more useful.

To really break even, the business must also include an amount of cost for the time and expertise of the owners. Often, particularly in small businesses, the owner fails to realise that, if they factored their own time in at a commercial rate, they would be making a loss.

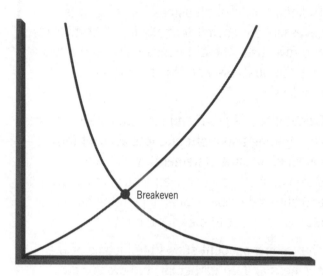

Breakeven

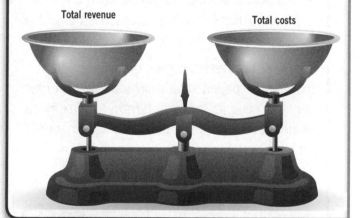

Total revenue · Total costs

✓ Maximise Your Marks

- Remember that 'what if?' scenarios can be run much more easily using a computer spreadsheet. With this method several different scenarios can be run, to see what will work best for the business.
- You must be able to accurately identify costs, and be aware of the different terms used for the same costs. Fixed and variable costs (and, by adding them together, total costs) are the most important.

❓ Test Yourself

1. Define 'fixed costs'.
2. What kind of costs are fixed costs, and what other name is given to them?
3. Define 'variable costs'.
4. What is meant by breakeven and how is it calculated?
5. Explain how you would calculate breakeven using the contribution method.

⭐ Stretch Yourself

1. Why might the idea of breakeven have limited uses to certain businesses?
2. What important factor might sometimes be forgotten when calculating breakeven?

Understanding Accounts

Trading, Profit and Loss Accounts

To know how well a business is doing, it is necessary to account formally for all of its costs and revenues. The difference between the two tells the business whether it is making a profit or a loss.

Calculations of profit and loss are usually shown on a **trading and profit and loss account** (also called an **income statement**), which lets all stakeholders know how well a business is doing and shows the operational side of the business. Managers use it to plan for the future.

The **trading account** shows the income of the business and, in particular, turnover – now called **sales revenue**. From this has to be taken the 'cost of sales' – in other words, how much it costs to make products. **Gross profit** is the amount of profit before expenses, such as wages, rent and power are taken off, to leave net or **operating profit**.

The **appropriation section** shows where the operating profit has gone. Some of this is taxation, some may be given to shareholders as dividends, and some may be kept to help the finances of the business.

	£
Turnover (sales)	400 000
less Cost of sales	240 000
Gross profit	160 000
Admin expenses	40 000
Selling costs	20 000
Net profit	100 000

💡 Boost Your Memory

Remember how 'cost of sales' works by doing a simple example. If you buy ten pencils at 8p each and sell them at 10p each, your revenue is $10 \times 10p = £1$ and your cost of sales is $10 \times 8p = 80p$. Your gross profit is 20p. Take out 10p for your time and the operating (net) profit is 10p.

Ratios

Ratios are important tools in business. They can show whether the business is in a strong or weak position and, from year to year, they can be used to make comparisons. A ratio is one thing measured in terms of another, often expressed as a percentage to make comparisons easier. Typical ratios used in business are:

- **Profitability ratios**, including the **profit margin**. This is calculated by (operating) profit ÷ sales × 100, to give a percentage, and it shows a business how much profit is being made per £1 of sales. Another profitability ratio is **return on capital employed** (**ROCE**) – how much profit is being generated compared to investment.
- **Liquidity ratios** look at how easily a business can pay its short-term debts from its assets. This is called the **current ratio** or **working capital ratio**.
- The **acid test** ratio is a harder test of ability to cover debts. It takes inventories out of the calculation, as these are not yet sold.

Different businesses expect different profit margins. A 'pound shop', for example, will have very low margins but high turnover. A luxury car business may have low sales but high margins on each car they sell.

✓ Maximise Your Marks

You should be able to both work out and interpret profitability ratios. You will not be expected to remember formulae, but you will be given them by most examination boards. Once you have worked out a ratio, however, you should be able to say whether this is good or bad for the business. A current ratio of between 1.5 : 1 and 3 : 1 is considered healthy. An acid test ratio of between 1 : 1 to 1.5 : 1 is OK.

These figures are only a rough rule of thumb, though; whether the ratio is 'good' or not can depend on the nature of the business.

Increasing Profitability

Managers and owners can try to increase profitability by increased efficiency, by raising revenue or by cutting costs. The business could try to:

- Make labour or machinery more productive (perhaps better motivated staff, new machines, better use of existing machines).
- Increase revenue by raising price. There is a danger that this may not work, though; if customers reduce the amount they buy, it could mean a fall in revenue. Sometimes a lower price will increase revenue, providing customers buy more. Businesses need to know their market and how customers will react to a price change.

- cut costs, for instance by reducing the labour force. However, this could cause problems such as leaving the remaining workers overworked and inefficient.

New machinery can decrease costs

Finance and Accounts

✓ Maximise Your Marks

- Remember, if it comes up in the exam, that **stakeholders** use the profit and loss account to compare profitability with previous periods and with other businesses. Managers, in particular, use it for future planning for the business.
- You should be able to make judgements by extracting figures from accounts to calculate ratios. When working with financial accounts, you will often be asked to calculate. To make sure that you get the full range of marks for your technique, you should always show your workings.

ⓘ Boost Your Memory

There are only three ways to increase profitability. Remember **RPC** for *Revenue, Productivity* and *Costs*.

❓ Test Yourself

1. Explain who would use the profit and loss account and what they would use it for.
2. What is meant by 'cost of sales'?
3. Give three examples of a business's expenses.
4. List three ways that a business can try to increase profitability.
5. Why might raising prices not increase profitability?

★ Stretch Yourself

1. Explain what a liquidity ratio shows.
2. How could you work out a profit margin, and what does it show?
3. Why do different businesses expect different profit margins?

Using the Balance Sheet

The Balance Sheet

The **balance sheet** lets all stakeholders know the wealth of a business. It shows what the business owns as against what it owes. It therefore measures **assets** (owns) against **liabilities** (owes). It will always balance, as the liabilities have been used to buy the assets.

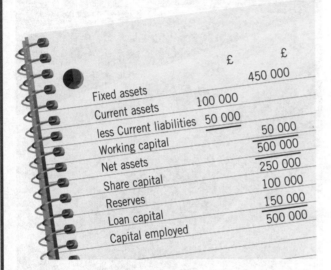

	£	£
Fixed assets		450 000
Current assets	100 000	
less Current liabilities	50 000	
Working capital		50 000
Net assets		500 000
Share capital		250 000
Reserves		100 000
Loan capital		150 000
Capital employed		500 000

Stakeholders use the balance sheet to judge the financial position of a business. Managers then use it to recommend possible courses of action to improve performance. The balance sheet is often called a '**snapshot**' as it shows the situation at the point at which it was taken. It can change very quickly.

It is called a **balance** sheet because both sides must be **equal**. This is because they are measuring the same things. Think about what you own and owe. Maybe you have a phone, an MP3 player, a bike or a favourite piece of clothing. These are your **assets** – what you own. The amounts that you had to earn or borrow in order to be able to buy those assets must equal what you paid for them. These amounts are your **liabilities**. It is the same with a business, with the important difference that the business is more likely to use **debt** to buy assets.

⚡ Boost Your Memory

If you think about what you have bought, against what it cost you to buy these things, you will see that the two totals must be equal – hence, a balance.

Using a Balance Sheet

A business needs the figures on the balance sheet in order to be able to work out **current** and **acid test** ratios.

Fixed assets (non-current), current assets and current liabilities will be shown, and the amount of stock (inventories) held will also be included. By looking at the balance sheet, you should therefore be able to work out the acid test ratio and make judgements about the state of health of the business.

✓ Maximise Your Marks

Remember that the balance sheet can change very quickly. For example, if a business had current assets that were mostly stock of finished goods, and then sold these, this would affect both assets and liabilities.

Reading a Balance Sheet

The main parts of the balance sheet show the assets of the business and its liabilities. The assets are divided into two types:

- Fixed assets (now called **non-current** assets), which are those that it is harder to turn into cash – such as land, buildings and machinery used in production. These assets are therefore less **liquid**.
- **Current** assets, which are those that are easier to turn into cash (more liquid). These include, for example, stocks (now called inventories) of finished goods that are ready to be sold.

Liabilities are all the things that a business owes. These are divided into:

- **Current liabilities**, which are debts that must be paid back within a year, such as bank overdrafts or creditors.
- **Long-term liabilities** (or **non-current liabilities**), are those having more than a year before they must be repaid, such as mortgages and long-term loans.

Liquidity measures how close an asset is to cash. The most liquid asset is cash, while the least liquid is likely to be buildings or land that it would be difficult to sell to turn into cash.

Assets *minus* liabilities gives what the business is worth at this moment. This is called **net current assets**.

The final part of the account shows how the money for net current assets was raised. This could be shareholders' funds (**total equity**), profit, or profit made in previous periods (**reserves**).

Both sides will always balance

❓ Test Yourself

1. What does a balance sheet show?
2. Explain why a balance sheet always balances.
3. What is the difference between non-current and current assets?
4. What is the difference between non-current and current liabilities?

★ Stretch Yourself

1. Which two important ratios need the balance sheet in order for a company to work them out?
2. How would you measure what the business is worth at any particular moment?
3. What is usually shown on the final part of the accounts?

Managing Cashflow

Cashflow

A business has a constant flow of cash in and out. Cash comes in through sales revenue and flows out to pay for costs.

A business needs enough cash to meet its day-to-day needs. The problem with cash is that the flows of it into and out of a business are never equal, so the business needs to manage them.

The business can forecast future inflows and outflows. It can plan solutions for forecast cash surpluses or deficits. A **cashflow** forecast is a planning tool that helps the business to see if it will have too much or too little cash for its needs.

💡 Boost Your Memory

A good way to think of the cashflow of a business is as a bucket being filled with water – but one with a hole in it. As fast as water (cash) comes in the top, it leaks out at the bottom. The business needs to make sure that the bucket never empties!

Why Cashflow is Important

One of the main reasons for business failure is a lack of cash for current needs. Even if a business looks healthy, with full order books and profitable trading, it cannot survive if it cannot pay its immediate bills for things like fuel and wages, or raw materials.

If there is more cash coming in than the business needs, this is called a cash **surplus**. If there is less cash than it needs, this is called a cash **shortage** or **deficit**.

Having too much cash can be as bad as not having enough. This is because the cash does not earn any **return**. Excess cash should therefore be turned into an asset that brings a return; it should be made to work by buying assets or investments. Even a bank deposit account is better than excess cash because it is earning **interest**.

✓ Maximise Your Marks

Remember that cash to pay bills is really important to a business. If it cannot pay its power bills, for instance, then power could be cut off. However healthy its order books, it cannot continue to trade and it becomes **insolvent** – unable to pay its debts.

Cashflow Forecasts

A **cashflow forecast** is a tool that is used to help the business to avoid problems. It looks at predicted flows of cash in and out of the business.

Cashflow forecasts help a business to know:
- when it will be short of cash and will need to borrow extra
- where it will have a cash surplus and can therefore invest cash in assets, bringing returns.

Forecasts are usually made from week to week or month to month. Comparisons with previous statements for similar periods can also help with accuracy.

Managers can use ICT in the form of software such as **spreadsheets** to help them in the construction of forecasts.

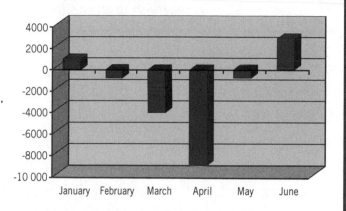

Managing Cashflow

Managers need to even out **inflows** and **outflows** so that there is always enough cash. Cash could be tied up in stock or in sales made on credit. Techniques to even out cashflows include:
- spreading payments, for example making monthly payments for power rather than paying annually
- rescheduling payments – paying a bill at a later date or using short-term credit
- arranging to receive revenue more regularly, for example getting customers to pay in instalments
- arranging to receive revenue early, for example persuading customers to pay in advance or pay deposits
- deciding to run down the stock they have rather than add to it.

Any method that leads to cash coming in early, or payments being made later, will help the cashflows of a business.

✓ Maximise Your Marks

- Remember that many cost reductions may have negative knock-on effects on the business. Examples include cutting back on staff, buying cheaper materials, cutting down on advertising and holding less stock. These can all cause problems.
- Cashflow forecasts are easy to construct and show periods of cash deficits or surpluses clearly if a graph is drawn. You must make sure that any suggestions you make are appropriate for the case study business.

❓ Test Yourself

1. Explain what is meant by the cashflow of a business.
2. What are the main streams of cash flowing into and out of a business?
3. How would a business use a cashflow forecast?
4. Suggest two ways of managing costs.
5. Suggest two ways of managing revenue.

★ Stretch Yourself

1. Define the terms 'cash surplus' and 'cash deficit'.
2. Why, for a business, can having too much cash be as bad as having too little?

Practice Questions

 Complete these exam-style questions to test your understanding. Check your answers on pages 94–95. You may wish to answer these questions on a separate piece of paper.

Knowledge Questions

Answer questions 1–10 first, then read the case study before answering the other questions. Each knowledge question is worth 1 mark. For these questions, put a ring around the letter of the correct answer.

1 Which of these would *not* even out cashflow?

   a) monthly payments rather than an annual bill **b**) better credit terms with suppliers

   c) excess cash kept in a secure place on the premises

   d) rescheduling payments to fall due at a later date.

2 Which of the following would be a suitable source of finance for a small start-up business?

   a) retained profit **b**) mortgage **c**) issuing shares **d**) owner's funds.

3 Fixed costs are costs that

   a) do not change **b**) change with output **c**) do not change with output **d**) do not change very much.

4 Revenue is:

   a) price × number sold **b**) price × fixed costs **c**) fixed costs × variable costs

   d) fixed costs + variable costs.

5 Which of the following is most likely to be an example of a variable cost?

   a) rent **b**) rates **c**) raw materials **d**) telephone lines.

6 The breakeven sales point is the point at which what is made?

   a) sales **b**) a profit **c**) a loss **d**) neither profit nor loss.

7 Which of the following can managers use to improve profitability?

   a) increase prices so revenue decreases **b**) lower prices so revenue increases

   c) sack some employees so the rest have to work harder **d**) keep existing machinery.

8 Which financial tool would usually include a prediction of borrowing requirements?

   a) breakeven chart **b**) balance sheet **c**) cashflow forecast **d**) profit and loss account.

9 Less cash coming in than the business needs is a:

   a) cash surplus **b**) revenue surplus **c**) cost overrun **d**) cash deficit.

10 Debts that must be repaid within a year are:

   a) non-current liabilities **b**) long-term liabilities **c**) current liabilities **d**) current problems.

Case Study

Ali and Eddie run a small printing company called Kwyk-Print, whose main business is printing programmes for local football clubs. They also print school brochures and advertising material such as catalogues for shops. They buy inks and paper from a wholesaler and employ two drivers who deliver finished materials. Their profitability ratio (measured as sales/profit) is currently 15 per cent, which is reasonable for a printing business of this size. Ali thinks that they can increase this ratio if they buy a new printing machine that is more efficient than their old one. The machine will cost £15,000.

Eddie is not sure they can buy it now as they already have a cash deficit forecast for the next three months. However, Ali thinks that he can solve this.

Application Questions

11 Outline the main costs and revenues for this business. (10)

12 Give two methods Ali and Eddie might have used to finance the business at start-up. (4)

13 What is a profitability ratio and why is it important to Kwyk-Print? (4)

Analysis and Evaluation Questions

14 Explain why breakeven would be of limited use to Kwyk-Print. (5)

15 Ali thinks he can solve the cashflow problem. Suggest ways by which he could do so. (5)

16 The new machine will cost £15,000. Ali and Eddie have the choice of: **a)** borrowing £15,000 from a family friend, for which he would want a shareholding; or **b)** borrowing £15,000 in a five year bank loan, secured on the machine.

By evaluating the advantages and disadvantages of each possible source, recommend which method they should use. (12)

How well did you do?

| 0–12 Try again | 13–25 Getting there | 26–38 Good work | 39–50 Excellent! |

Different Types of Market

Supply, Demand and Markets

Prices are decided by the operation of supply and demand:

- **Demand** is the amount a customer is willing to pay at a price.
- **Supply** is the amount a business is willing to sell at that price.

As price rises, demand tends to fall and supply tends to rise. Where the two meet is where the market agrees on price. This is called **equilibrium**.

A **market** is anywhere where a business and its customers come together to decide what to buy and sell, and at what price. A market does not have to have a physical existence (like a farmers' market), but can take place via telephone or online.

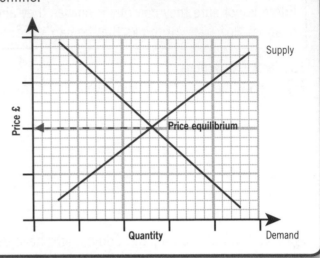

Competitive Markets

Some markets have a number of competing businesses. Very **competitive markets** have lots of businesses, and competition tends to bring lower prices. It is usually assumed that competition automatically lowers prices and is better for consumers.

Businesses compete through better customer service, such as location and delivery, branding and advertising. Consumers have a choice of what to buy, and where from.

Governments encourage competition because of these benefits. Critics would argue that competition can lead to a lack of innovation and research, as there is no money for it, so products do not develop or improve.

💡 Boost Your Memory

It may help to understand a competitive market if you imagine a traditional market for something like eggs, with many egg sellers. All the eggs are the same, and will be the same price, but stalls can compete on packaging, advertising and even on being nice to customers.

Monopolies

Monopolies are markets in which there is little competition. A monopoly in the UK is considered to be any business with 25 per cent share of their market.

Monopolies usually mean higher prices and limited consumer choice, but monopolies are able to develop new products and innovations.

Monopolies can build barriers to entry into their market, such as legal barriers like patents or restrictive practices like agreeing prices or contracts with suppliers.

Other barriers include the amount of initial investment needed (e.g. coffee plantations) or high advertising spend and strong brands.

Monopolies are generally thought of as being bad for consumers, leading to higher prices and less choice, but often it is the higher profits that allow businesses to develop new products.

Commodity Markets

Commodities are crops and raw materials produced in **bulk**. They include coal, wheat, rice, copper, coffee, oil, sugar, aluminium and steel.

Sugar from one country is no different to sugar from another, so there is one worldwide price for a commodity.

Commodities are traded in huge amounts, in organised markets with strict rules. Demand is not just for now, but for the future. Supply is hard to change.

In the market are big businesses that must secure supplies for the future, as well as speculators gambling on future prices. Small businesses are affected by commodity prices; for example, bakers use wheat, plumbers use copper and all use fuel and energy.

Commodities are transported in huge amounts via container ships

✓ Maximise Your Marks

- Almost all businesses rely on commodities (even if it is only the oil that is used for petrol), so all are vulnerable to changes in commodity prices. The important thing to remember is that these changes are outside their control, so businesses just have to accept them and cope.

- The operation of demand and supply in a market is unlikely to be asked as a specific question, but you can bring it into other questions. Saying, for example, that 'an increase in the demand for *x* pushed prices up' shows a good level of technical knowledge.

Becoming a Monopoly

Businesses can grow to be monopolies through takeovers and mergers. The UK **Competition Commission** judges whether or not mergers and takeovers are in the public interest.

Many businesses try to make themselves stand out in the market by trying some of the tricks of monopolies; they try to make their products or services unique, brand themselves (brands are powerful ways to control markets) and use advertising and promotion.

However, each of these has a cost, so it may be that prices have to be higher to pay for them, or profits lower.

❓ Test Yourself

1. Explain the operation of supply and demand.
2. Describe a competitive market.
3. Explain what is meant by a monopoly.
4. Give three barriers to entry that monopolies can build.
5. What is meant by a 'commodity' and why are their prices important to small businesses?

⭐ Stretch Yourself

1. Explain how businesses can try to compete using the sort of barriers that monopolies build.
2. Why can using such tactics lead to a loss of custom?

Global Competition

International Trade

International trade means that countries can exchange goods that they are able to produce with those that other countries produce. Without it, many products that we take for granted would not be available. Both countries gain, providing production is in the country that is relatively more efficient.

International trade is in visibles and invisibles.
- **Visibles** are goods that can be seen or touched.
- **Invisibles** are services such as insurance or transport.

Products entering a country are **imports** and those leaving it are **exports**. Countries may protect their own markets by subsidising exports, taxing imports or through tariffs or quotas.

✓ Maximise Your Marks

To decide if a product is an import or export, visible or invisible, ask two questions. Firstly, does it deal in goods or services (visible or invisible)? Secondly, which way does the payment go? The product must have gone in the opposite direction to the payment.

Globalisation

Globalisation describes how competition in many industries is now on a global scale rather than just national. This can lead to better and cheaper products, and more choice, but also means that businesses are increasingly dependent on each other. Globalisation has good and bad effects. Good effects include:
- Global brands mean that consumers get the same quality for the same good anywhere in the world.
- Businesses can keep costs down.
- Businesses can gain cheaper supplies and a larger market.

Bad effects include:
- Global businesses can choose to produce in countries with cheaper labour and pay tax in countries with lower taxation rates, but this can give them a poor reputation.
- Local businesses cannot compete, so consumer choice is reduced.
- If one global brand destroys competition, choice may be limited and prices rise.

Globally, there are a few rich countries and many poor ones. Globalisation may see businesses taking advantage of this unequal income distribution, but they may face more competition.

♀ Boost Your Memory

There are many well-known global brands that you can use in examples. Think about such a product (e.g. Coca-Cola) and this will help you remember what's good and bad about globalisation.

Multinationals

Many global businesses are **multinationals**. A multinational is a business that has operations and bases in many countries, often formed by **mergers** or **takeovers**. Some businesses (like the oil industry) are almost bound to be multinationals, because of the processes involved and the investment needed.

Multinationals gain from being big. They can buy in bulk and even control supplies. They can locate where costs and taxes are lowest and where laws are least likely to affect them. They also establish **global brands**. Brands are of immense value to a business, helping it to be recognised and to gain new markets.

Many multinationals are organised as **holding companies** that hold shares in other companies in the same group. This means the companies are part of a global brand but can keep their local or national identities.

Benefits and Drawbacks of Multinationals

Multinationals, with factories and operations in many different countries, may be able to take advantage of poorer countries. They may operate in places with lower labour costs, less strict labour laws, fewer rules and regulations or lower tax.

Human rights groups have sometimes accused them of exploiting child or cheap labour or natural resources in poor countries.

Multinationals have been accused of destroying the environment and even of political interference, supporting certain governments and opposing others for their own advantage.

Some multinationals, though, have been congratulated for bringing work, development and wealth to poorer countries.

✓ Maximise Your Marks

- If you're aiming for the highest marks, there are links that you can make between international trade, globalisation and multinationals, with good and bad points for each.
- There are many issues attached to international trade, globalisation and multinationals. There are always two sides to the argument and you must weigh up both. For example, some people see **free trade** (trade without restrictions) as a force for good. Others see it as destroying the chances of developing countries to compete.

❓ Test Yourself

1. Explain what is meant by international trade.
2. What is the difference between visible imports and exports and invisible ones?
3. What is meant by a 'multinational'?
4. What is meant by 'holding companies'?

⭐ Stretch Yourself

1. Explain what is meant by globalisation.
2. Outline how globalisation can be good or bad for businesses and consumers.
3. Explain some of the benefits and drawbacks of multinationals.

Ethical and Environmental Issues

Understanding the Context of Business

Ethical Issues

Being **ethical** means doing the right or moral thing. Examples of ethical practice in business include not testing products on animals, paying fair prices for materials and skills, not using cheap or child labour and not operating in dirty or dangerous conditions.

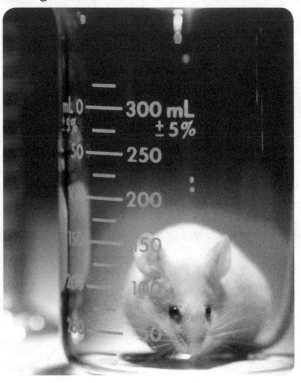

Is this ethical?

Acting in an ethical way is often attractive to customers, so it helps to bring about customer loyalty. Customers prefer to buy products that have been sourced and produced in an ethical manner, so being ethical can help profits.

Many investors in businesses, including shareholders, will only invest in those that have ethical policies. This is called **ethical investment**.

✓ Maximise Your Marks

To help you understand what ethical behaviour is, think of all the business practices that people might object to – things like using child labour in the clothing industry, or testing cosmetics on animals. Ethical practice is not making a profit from exploiting someone or something.

Environmental Issues

Businesses can create **environmental problems**, including waste, noise and pollution. Modern businesses manage these with environmental policies (sometimes termed '**corporate social responsibility**' or **CSR**), designed to show that they care about these issues.

Many businesses aim for **sustainable** production. This means ensuring that anything taken from the environment during production is replaced. They also use more renewable resources and alternative technologies, such as wind and solar power.

Carbon footprint measures the impact business operations have on the environment. Businesses try to reduce this by **recycling**, using inputs from **sustainable resources**, controlling pollution, using greener fuels and adopting energy saving policies. The Government uses tax and laws to control environmental problems.

Green is Good

Environmental policies and practices are also referred to as '**green**' policies. Anything that helps preserve the environment is considered to be green. There are even green technologies.

Green policies are not only good for the planet, but good for business. Green businesses are seen as positive, so customers stay loyal.

Green policies (like recycling and green fuels) may also cut costs. Despite this, in some cases, businesses charge higher prices and thus make higher profits, with the excuse that being good or green brings higher costs.

Pressure Groups

Pressure groups are groups of people or organisations that try to influence businesses and governments to act in ethical or environmental ways. Well-known pressure groups include the environmental group Greenpeace, the World Wide Fund For Nature (formerly known as the World Wildlife Fund), PETA (People for the Ethical Treatment of Animals) and many charities. Pressure groups often use publicity gained from stunts to get their message across.

Pressure groups may also reveal when businesses are acting unethically. They have challenged governments and major companies by publicising whale hunts, exposing child or cheap labour used in production and finding dangerous working conditions or other unethical or environmentally damaging practices.

Some pressure groups are set up to cope with a single issue – against the building of a railway, for example, or in favour of a bypass. Others (like Greenpeace) focus on any environmental issues that arise.

Greenpeace protests against killing whales in Iceland

✓ Maximise Your Marks

You can gain extra marks by showing that you can use up-to-date and relevant examples to support your answers. Look in your local newspaper for issues that are making the news and use these if you can.

Social Costs and Benefits

Businesses bring **social costs** and **social benefits** to the communities where they operate:

- Social **costs** are problems carried by society as a whole. The main social costs created by businesses are pollution, waste and congestion due to increased transport.
- Social **benefits** are gains shared by everyone. Social benefits can include making provision for the local community – such as leisure and recreation facilities, social events, sports or team sponsorship, supporting local schools or educational and training opportunities.

Social costs and benefits are caused by business but shared by the whole of the community where the business operates. Smart businesses try to ensure that social benefits outweigh costs.

Businesses that bring social benefits will gain increased custom from a better reputation.

❓ Test Yourself

1. Using an example, state what is meant by 'being ethical'.

2. Using an example, state what is meant by 'being environmental'.

3. What is meant by 'corporate social responsibility'?

4. Giving an example for each, state the difference between social costs and social benefits.

⭐ Stretch Yourself

1. Explain how 'green' policies can both be good for the business as well as for the environment, and lead to higher profits.

2. What is a pressure group, and what do pressure groups do?

Government and EU Influence

Government Spending and Taxation

Businesses are affected by changes in government spending, taxation and laws.

Government spending is on services such as education, transport and the NHS. This can boost businesses and the economy.

Westminster

Taxation can affect the ability of businesses to survive and compete.

- Taxes on consumers will affect demand. An increase in income tax will make consumers worse off, so they may spend less. An increase in VAT makes the price of products higher.
- Taxes on business profit may also discourage businesses.

Laws to **protect workers**, change working conditions or make working lives better (minimum wage, paternity/maternity leave, health and safety laws) can also bring increased costs to businesses, especially small ones.

Interest Rates

Interest rates are the price of borrowing money. In the UK, they are not set by the Government but by the Bank of England, so that political parties cannot change them in order to bring about economic change that could help them win elections.

If interest rates are high, or increase, it becomes more expensive to borrow money. This affects both businesses and consumers.

Bank of England

Small businesses that rely on overdrafts, bank loans and credit terms will find it more expensive to borrow at higher interest rates. They may not be able to hold as much stock, or as wide a range, as they would want to, as higher interest rates increase their costs. They may also not be able to offer credit terms to customers.

Consumers may also spend less. Many consumers have debt – especially mortgages – so higher interest rates reduce their ability to purchase, especially luxury goods.

🔔 Boost Your Memory

Look around you to remember some of the many things that government spends money on, including roads, schools, health services, social services and benefits.

How the EU Has Affected Business

Many EU countries decided that it would be easier for businesses if all were using the same currency. This currency, the **euro**, was introduced in 1999.

It benefits business (and travellers) by making currency changes unnecessary. This makes trade easier and smoother.

The UK government decided not to join the single currency because it felt its own currency was stronger than the euro, and that joining it would mean losing some control over economic policies.

The **Maastricht Treaty** of 1991 was written to encourage all EU countries to work within the same rules. It included the **Social Chapter** which, along with setting a minimum wage and maximum working hours, said that:

- all workers have the right to join a trades union
- men and women should be treated equally at work
- workers could become involved on the boards of businesses
- EU citizens should have the right to work in any EU country.

✓ Maximise Your Marks

- Remember that the EU is a powerful trading bloc with its own institutions, such as the European Parliament, so it can sometimes take decisions that go against national interests.
- With many questions you will be asked to look at both sides of an argument. For example, the EU has brought many benefits, such as trade and the Social Chapter. But it has also brought in new rules to which some businesses object. You must weigh up both sides in the context of the case study business before making a decision.

The European Union

The **European Union** (EU) is currently 27 countries in Europe who have agreed to act together on a number of issues.

- It provides businesses within it with a larger market (the **single market**) of over 500 million people.
- It has introduced common measurements and a common currency, both of which help business.
- It allows free movement of goods and workers within its borders.
- It provides grants and subsidies to help businesses and poorer countries within it. European Regional Policy helps regions facing economic problems.
- The European Social Fund pays for retraining workers and programmes to help businesses.
- Funding is also available to help develop transport and services.

❓ Test Yourself

1. Suggest three major government influences on business.
2. Explain how changes in taxation can affect businesses.
3. What is meant by 'the single market'?

⭐ Stretch Yourself

1. Explain how a change in interest rates might affect small businesses and consumers.
2. Give three changes introduced by the Social Chapter of the Maastricht Treaty.

External Economic Influences

External Influences

External influences are those that are outside the control of a business. They include major **economic factors** and **natural factors**, like disasters, poor harvests and disease in animals. The extent of the influence will be strongly linked to the type of market in which the business trades.

Bad weather and disease can destroy harvests

Population changes affect demand. The UK has an ageing population, with more people living longer. This puts a strain on the health service and on pensions. The UK also has a history of welcoming people from abroad. These bring benefits such as increased demand, new skills and a richer culture, but they also bring costs in terms of education and health.

For each business, a different external factor or set of factors will be important, dependent on the market in which the business operates. A business running old people's homes, for example, would benefit from an ageing population; one selling teenage fashions might suffer.

Foreign Exchange

Where the UK is concerned, **exchange rates** are how much the UK pound (£) is worth in terms of other currencies like the US dollar ($) or the EU euro (€). Any business that trades in different countries has to pay its bills in the currency of that country. This means that it has to buy that currency.

The strength of the UK economy (and that of other countries) is linked to how much of another currency each £1 buys. A higher value pound means that more foreign currency can be bought. A lower value pound has the opposite effect.

The UK's main trading partners are the European Union (accounting for more than 50 per cent of UK exports and imports) and the USA, so the strength of the pound against the euro and the US dollar are the most important.

Changes in exchange rates will actually change the price of certain goods and services. When the value of the pound goes up and down, so does the price of imports and exports.

Imagine that the cost of buying wheat from America is $100 a ton. If the exchange rate is $1 = £0.75, then the UK importer must spend £75 to buy $100 to buy the wheat. If the rate changes to, say, $1 = £0.80, the price is now £80 a ton because the importer must spend £80 to buy $100.

✓ Maximise Your Marks

To be sure that you are making the right decisions, always look at the case study business in terms of the market it is in. Which factor or factors do you think is/are most important to it?

Business Cycles

Changes to the economy tend to happen in **economic cycles** that go from **'boom' to 'bust'** via 'recovery' and 'recession'.

Boom years have high levels of consumer spending and low levels of unemployment. At the top of the boom, there will be rising wages and rising prices. Businesses will find it harder to meet increased demand, and prices rise.

This leads to a **downturn**. Demand falls, interest rates tend to rise and unemployment increases. Businesses may find it harder to borrow money, which can be a particular problem for small businesses.

Eventually, prices fall, employment rises and the economy picks up. This is called a **recovery**.

Governments can try to iron out 'boom and bust' by changing patterns of public spending – for example, increasing public spending if private sector spending is falling.

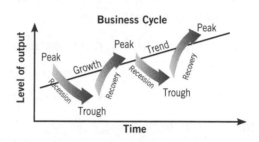

Economic Growth

Economic growth measures **production** and **expenditure** in an economy. It shows whether the economy is heading for boom or bust.
- **Positive** growth means strong demand. This is generally good for businesses.
- **Negative** or **zero** growth means weak demand.
- Two quarters of negative growth together is officially a **recession**. This is bad for businesses and many struggle to survive.

Small businesses are likely to be badly affected by a recession, but this depends on the type of market in which the business operates. Providers of luxury products may find buyers putting off spending decisions. Those selling necessities are likely to suffer least.

Recession leads to business failure

✓ Maximise Your Marks

Remember, if you have a question about this topic, that small businesses often don't have the funds or the assets to be able to withstand a serious recession, and business failure is common in this part of the cycle.

❓ Test Yourself

1. What is meant by external influences?
2. How can changes in the age of the population affect businesses?
3. Explain what happens in a 'boom' year of a business cycle.
4. What does economic growth measure?

⭐ Stretch Yourself

1. Explain why the foreign exchange value of the UK pound is important.
2. How do changes in exchange rates affect the value of imports and exports?
3. If the pound/euro exchange rate changed from €1.60 = £1.00 to €1.50 = £1.00, what would be the effect on a UK grocer importing €80 worth of French apples?

Practice Questions

Complete these exam-style questions to test your understanding. Check your answers on page 95. You may wish to answer these questions on a separate piece of paper.

Knowledge Questions

Answer questions 1–10 first, then read the case study before answering the other questions. Each knowledge question is worth 1 mark.

In the following questions, fill in the spaces with the correct term.

1 A .... is anywhere where a business and its customers come together to decide on what to buy and sell and the price to be paid.

2 In the UK if a business has a .... market share, it is considered to be a monopoly.

3 Costs that affect the whole community, such as pollution, are called ....

4 Crops and raw materials produced in bulk are called ....

5 The sale of a service from the UK to the USA would be an .... import to the USA.

6 Businesses with factories and operations in many different countries are called ....

7 A business policy that covers environmental and ethical issues is called ...., often shortened to CSR.

8 Organisations that campaign for particular causes or changes are called ....

9 Economic activity charts levels of .... and output in the economy as a whole.

10 When growth is either zero or negative for two consecutive periods this is a ....

Case Study

Baseline make flat screen TV sets and have a 10 per cent market share in a market with over a dozen other competitors. Their sets are more expensive than the competition, because they insist on making them with ethical and environmental safeguards in place. They are also pledged to reduce their carbon footprint.

The raw materials that go into making TV sets are often extracted in difficult and dangerous conditions, sometimes by child labour, so Baseline buys from other sources. It imports materials from South America, manufactures the sets in Nottingham, then exports them around the world. Purchasers of the sets can buy an online assistance package.

Application Questions

11 Using an example from the case study, state what is meant by an ethical policy. (4)

....

....

....

....

12 What imports and exports are Baseline involved in? (6)

13 Explain the possible benefits to the consumer of a market such as the one in which Baseline operates. (4)

Analysis and Evaluation Questions

14 Suggest how Baseline could reduce its carbon footprint. (8)

15 Evaluate why being ethical and environmental is also good business practice for Baseline. (8)

How well did you do?

| 0–10 | Try again | 11–20 | Getting there | 21–30 | Good work | 31–40 | Excellent! |

Answers

Starting and Organising a Business

Pages 6–7 Starting a Business Enterprise
Test Yourself Answers
1. A need is necessary for survival; a want is anything other than this.
2. Businesses compete through better quality, convenience, good design or establishing brands.
3. You must justify your decision, for example, brands are more important because they make customers loyal to a business.
4. To find out about competition to better help them compete.

Stretch Yourself Answers
1. Possible reasons are to supply goods and services and to make a profit.
2. A business that aims to provide a service to a community for reasons other than making a profit.
3. Where a demand for a good or service exists, but it is not currently being met by an existing business.

Pages 8–9 Enterprise and Entrepreneurs
Test Yourself Answers
1. Enterprise is when a person takes a business risk in order to gain a reward, which is usually the profit made by the business.
2. Someone with enterprise skills who carries the risk of starting a business and providing its organisation.
3. Invention, innovation and protection.
4. Making a conscious effort to be creative.

Stretch Yourself Answers
1. Teamwork, organisation, problem solving, networking, energy, communication skills and being able to keep an overview.
2. This is when an entrepreneur asks a 'what if?' question such as 'What if a new competitor enters the market?'
3. By making it possible for 'what if?' situations to be modelled on spreadsheets.

Pages 10–11 Stakeholders
Test Yourself Answers
1. Those people, groups or organisations that have a stake, or interest, in the performance of a business.
2. Because they have a direct interest in the success of the business.
3. Stakeholders who have a less direct interest in a business.
4. Examples include customers, suppliers, banks, the government, pressure groups and the communities in which the business operates.

Stretch Yourself Answers
1. Examples: owners may want higher profits but customers want lower prices or suppliers may want to be paid at once whereas owners want time to pay.
2. Any solution suggested (such as borrowing money to pay suppliers now) should solve the problem.
3. Owners aim for success and profit; pressure groups try to bring about change; customers want quality and reliability; suppliers want to sell their products and be paid; banks and other financial stakeholders want a return on lending; government wants taxes; the community wants jobs.

Pages 12–13 Setting Business Aims and Objectives
Test Yourself Answers
1. Aims say what the business wants to achieve in the long run. They are long-term goals towards which the business can work.
2. Because they are often not very precise.
3. Targets that are Specific, Measurable, Achievable, Realistic and Time-related.
4. Survival.

Stretch Yourself Answers
1. Objectives are like stepping stones used to reach the aims.
2. These include the independence of working for yourself or the pleasure of job satisfaction – knowing that this is 'a job well done'.
3. Aims and objectives; methods, staff and products it intends to use to try to achieve the aims; financial details and forecasts; the direction that the business will take.

Pages 14–15 Business location
Test Yourself Answers
1. Some may need to deal with customers and be close to them, some need display space, others need good transport systems.
2. Examples: expense; attraction to customers; availability of specialist labour; closeness to competitors; reputation of area.
3. One that can locate anywhere.
4. Primary, secondary and tertiary.
5. Being near the source of raw materials, to keep down the cost of transporting them.

Stretch Yourself Answers
1. Bulk increasing means products become harder or more expensive to transport after processing or manufacture. Bulk decreasing means products become easier or cheaper to transport after processing or manufacture.
2. Different languages, laws, currency; local laws must be obeyed and business conducted in the language and currency of the host country.

Pages 16–17 Answers to Practice Questions
Answers to Knowledge Questions
1. c) **2.** a) **3.** b) **4.** a) **5.** b) **6.** b) **7.** c) **8.** b) **9.** d) **10.** b)

Answers to Application Questions
11. The internal stakeholders are Josh and Mary (2). The external stakeholders are their customers (1) and the community (1).
12. Josh and Mary's aims include wanting to be their own boss, using existing skills and earning an income (3). As the business grows, they may want breakeven (1), then a profit (1) and perhaps to grow bigger (1).
13. Snapz's USP is the complete service of photo, mounting and special framed print (2). Snapz adds value by providing convenience and quality (2).

Answers to Analysis and Evaluation Questions
14. The decision you make does not matter, it is the reasons to support it that do. The analysis is: the high street location will have display space (1) and attract customers (1), but it will cost more (1), whereas the low-cost location will save money (1), allow for web selling (1) but mean advertising costs (1). For example: you may think that the cost argument is most important because keeping costs down at the start is vital (2).

Structuring a Business

Pages 18–19 Structuring a Business
Test Yourself Answers
1. The smallest business with only one owner.
2. Partnerships are agreements between two or more people.
3. A company that has a small number of shareholders and cannot sell shares to the public.
4. Just start trading; no formal agreement or paperwork is necessary.
5. Companies carry the initials 'Ltd' or 'plc' after their name.

Stretch Yourself Answers
1. Liability is the legal term used for the responsibility of the owners of a business for the debts of that business; limited liability means responsibility for debt is limited to the amount invested in the business.
2. By the 'plc' and 'Ltd' in the name of the business.
3. Limited liability businesses may not be able to pay their debts, so banks may be less likely to lend to them without guarantees of some sort.

Pages 20–21 Larger Business Organisations
Test Yourself Answers
1. A limited liability company that sells shares to the public and is listed on the stock exchange.
2. Anyone can buy shares, including competitors.
3. The accounts of the business, its profits and forecasts for its future.
4. Businesses owned not by the public but by local or national government on behalf of the public.

Stretch Yourself Answers

1. They have to provide reports each year, which include details of finances and profits as well as their performance for the year.
2. They can give competitors a good idea of what is happening with the business, so helping them to compete.
3. A business with a social aim such as being fair or ethical.

Pages 22–23 Franchising
Test Yourself Answers

1. A way for a successful business to expand, and for other businesses to share in that success. The franchiser sells the right to use its business model to the franchiser.
2. The franchiser is the seller of the franchise that has a successful product, brand or format, providing ideas, support, training and advertising for the brand and the franchisee.
3. The franchisee is the business that buys into the success of the established business. It buys the use of its name, brand, advertising, reputation and support.
4. Franchisers charge a fee for the franchise and collect a royalty based on a percentage of the annual sales of the franchisee.

Stretch Yourself Answers

1. Franchising is a way of organising a business; ownership can be any one of a number of types.
2. A franchisee that is a limited company will have limited liability, so might not be able to guarantee to pay its debts.
3. The disadvantage to franchisees is lack of independence. A disadvantage to the franchiser is that a poor franchisee could harm their reputation.

Pages 24–25 Internal Organisational Structures
Test Yourself Answers

1. An organisation controlled from the centre, where decisions are made by a few people at the top of the organisation.
2. An organisation where decision-making is spread, so that better decisions are made at local level.
3. Managers and workers are shown in a hierarchy. Each manager has a span of control showing the number of workers under his or her control. The people underneath are called subordinates and the manager has authority over them.
4. A structure that is in layers, where the people at the top have more authority than those at the bottom.
5. Finance, human resources, marketing, production and administration.

Stretch Yourself Answers

1. A tall structure has many layers but few people at each layer. A flat structure has few layers and many people at each layer.
2. In a tall structure, communication between layers tends to be formal but can be slow. In a flat structure, communication both within and between layers is generally good.

Pages 26–27 Answers to Practice Questions
Answers to Knowledge Questions

1. a) 2. d) 3. b) 4. a) 5. b) 6. sole trader
7. liability 8. public 9. nationalised 10. tall

Answers to Application Questions

11. The main benefits to Kris of being a sole trader are that it is easy to set up (1), he makes all the decisions (1) and he keeps all the profits (1).
12. The main benefits of Kris going into partnership with Matt are Matt's additional expertise (1), shared decision-making (1), shared responsibility (1) and extra capital (1).
13. A franchise is when a successful business (1), in this case UKMTL, sells its brand and business model (1) to a buyer like Kris. UKMTL is the franchiser, Kris is the franchisee (2). Kris would pay UKMTL a fee (1) and a royalty (1) based on turnover (1). In return, Kris has guaranteed customers and national support (1).

Answers to Analysis and Evaluation Questions

14. Your actual decision does not matter as long as you use the advantages and disadvantages of sole traders and partnerships to support your judgement. For example, if Kris wants to maintain his independence (1), keep all of his profit (1) and take his own decisions (1), but also keep his own books (1), do his own marketing (1) and raise all his own capital (1), he will decide to be a sole trader.
15. Again, your actual decision does not matter. For example, a franchise provides guaranteed customers (1) and national support (1), but costs an initial fee (1) plus a royalty (1) and may limit Kris's independence (1).

Marketing and Customers

Pages 28–29 Understanding the Market
Test Yourself Answers

1. Age, income, lifestyle, location, sex and ethnicity.
2. Questionnaires, interviews, surveys, focus groups or watching customer behaviour.
3. Company reports, market reports, published resources, government statistics or the Internet.
4. Analysis that measures the internal Strengths and Weaknesses of the business against its external Opportunities and Threats.

Stretch Yourself Answers

1. Who will buy the product and how often; how much the customer will pay; where the customer will buy the product from; which other businesses are selling the product; what can be used to persuade the customer to buy.
2. The source, to see if it is reliable; the date, to see if it is recent; who commissioned the research, to see if it is likely to be biased.

Pages 30–31 The Marketing Mix: Product
Test Yourself Answers

1. The term given to the way that a business sells a product using the 'four Ps' of Product, Price, Place and Promotion.
2. The range of goods that a business sells.
3. Extra costs and extra competition.
4. Many people have bought the product but there are also many competitors.

Stretch Yourself Answers

1. A product that has a high market share in a fast growing, often new, market and needs a lot of promotion.
2. Usually they keep the cows, using the cash to support stars; keep the stars and try to turn them into cash cows; spend on the problem children to turn them into stars and sell off the dogs.
3. Extension strategies such as changes in advertising, packaging, renaming or re-branding or improving the product.

Pages 32–33 The Marketing Mix: Price
Test Yourself Answers

1. Sensitive: luxuries such as expensive holidays. Not sensitive: necessities such as bread and milk.
2. By adding up the various costs of the product and then adding on a percentage for profit (called a mark-up).
3. Because it is often difficult to work out exactly how much each product cost to make, transport, package, advertise, etc.
4. Businesses can try to increase growth and market share through skimming and penetration pricing, or sales through promotional pricing.

Stretch Yourself Answers

1. Penetration pricing to gain market share; loss leaders to attract customers who then buy other, profitable, products; promotional pricing to boost sales in the short term.
2. When customers want to be the first to own a new product.
3. Some price strategies only work with certain products. For example, a burger bar could not use skimming, as this is only effective for new technology products.

Pages 34–35 The Marketing Mix: Promotion
Test Yourself Answers
1. It is used to inform customers and to persuade them to buy products.
2. Point-of-sale material, leaflets, business cards, flyers and other information.
3. Small scale sponsorship – for example, of a local sports team.
4. Many businesses rely on their reputation and on 'word of mouth' recommendation.
5. National television or billboard campaigns, or the sponsorship of famous teams or national events.

Stretch Yourself Answers
1. It depends on the cost of the promotion. A promotion is only effective if the increase in sales is large enough to produce an increase in profit that is bigger than the cost.
2. The cost of the promotion, who it might reach, and what sort of service the market wants from the business.

Pages 36–37 The Marketing Mix: Place
Test Yourself Answers
1. It refers to where a product is sold ('place') and to how the product gets there ('distribution').
2. Because there are different costs involved and different markets targeted.
3. Retail outlets range from small corner shops to supermarkets, department stores and specialist stores.
4. The name given to buying and selling goods and services via the Internet.
5. Some products (such as music tracks and even movies) can be more easily distributed online than in physical form.

Stretch Yourself Answers
1. The business will be concerned with the cost of distribution, how it reaches its market and its profit. Customers are more concerned with convenience, delivery services, cost and reliability.
2. Products such as music and movie downloads, or services such as flights, train fares and holidays, as they have no delivery charges.

Pages 38–39 Customer Service
Test Yourself Answers
1. The level of service that matches customer expectations.
2. It helps to build customer loyalty. Customers who are happy will return and become repeat customers. It is much more efficient to retain customers than to keep having to attract new ones.
3. Providing information, giving accurate advice, having good after-sales service and providing convenience, such as a good location or different ways to pay.
4. Cards issued to customers that give 'points' or other offers.

Stretch Yourself Answers
1. Businesses should fill orders accurately, deliver on time and both listen to and act on any complaints. They should be open as stated, hold stock to meet demand and sell products that perform to the standards customers expect.
2. Businesses can set targets to reduce complaints, exchanges or refunds, or deal with customer concerns within a set time period. Progress towards these can then be measured.
3. The reputation of the business is often built on, or destroyed by, its after-sales service. Helping the customer with the product, or with problems, helps customer loyalty.

Pages 40–41 Consumer Protection
Test Yourself Answers
1. The laws and rules that are put in place to protect the consumer against bad practice by businesses.
2. Some laws protect the consumer from harm. Others protect against cheating, such as false information or incorrect pricing.
3. Being clear about charges and penalties and using accurate weights and measures.
4. The Sale of Goods and Supply of Services Act and the Trade Descriptions Act.
5. Because it covers all business sectors and activities and is more wide-ranging, for example providing protection for the more vulnerable.

Stretch Yourself Answers
1. It is a Latin phrase meaning 'let the buyer beware'. It means that customers have a responsibility to check quality for themselves; it is not all down to the business.
2. It means that the product does what it is meant to do.

Pages 42–43 Answers to Practice Questions
Answers to Knowledge Questions
1. c) 2. b) 3. d) 4. d) 5. b) 6. b) 7. a) 8. d) 9. a) 10. b)

Answers to Application Questions
11. Jurgen has done primary research (1) but only collected qualitative (1) data. This is up to date (1), but it is hard to interpret (1) and may be inaccurate (1), for example using the Internet (1).
12. Jurgen could carry out more primary research (1) on greater numbers (1), using methods like questionnaires (1). He could also carry out desk research (1).
13. ADD+ is at the launch stage (1) and this means costs can be high (1), as advertising (1) and distribution networks (1) are needed.

Answers to Analysis and Evaluation Questions
14. An example would be: the product is a good one, as it has been tested (1) and can be manufactured at low cost, so he should be able to sell it at a reasonable price (1). I would suggest a price strategy of skimming (1), as this is a new and technologically advanced product (1), and people who want to be first to try it will pay the higher price (1). In this way, he will only reach a small part of the market to begin with (1), which will give him time to build up a distribution network (1). I would suggest advertising that is targeted (1) at this high-income group.
15. If you decide on a national launch, you should talk about possible advertising and promotional campaigns (1) and their expense and effectiveness (1), along with the problems (1) that a lack of a distribution network (1) would cause for a product that is good/proven (1) and will be very popular if pitched at the right price (1).
16. If launching locally, Jurgen could use point-of-sale material (1), leaflets (1) and flyers (1). He could sponsor a local event or sports team (1). His most effective way would probably be flyers (1), because he could reach a set number of people (1).
    If launching nationally, he would need more expensive types of promotion (1), such as national TV (1) or billboard campaigns (1) and the sponsorship of famous teams or national events (1). His most effective method would be TV, which would reach a wide audience (1) but would be very expensive (1).

Human Resources

Pages 44–45 Managing Staff
Test Yourself Answers
1. The process by which a business finds new staff.
2. It starts with an advertisement. People apply with their work history (CV) and letters. Applicants are shortlisted and invited to an interview. The best candidate is then offered the job.
3. On the grounds of gender, race, religion, creed, sexual orientation, disability or age.
4. People working more effectively because they want to, or sometimes linked to a reward.

Stretch Yourself Answers
1. If the change is managed well, there will be increased efficiency as workers will stay motivated. Badly managed change can lead to problems and demotivated workers.
2. Valuing the work they do, for example through promotion; staff development; good working conditions; flexible working practices.

Pages 46–47 Methods of Payment
Test Yourself Answers
1. The way a worker is paid.
2. A wage is linked to the work done or time spent at work. A salary is an annual amount paid monthly and is not linked to hours worked or tasks completed.
3. Piece rates, time rates and commission.
4. According to qualifications, skill and experience; or in order to retain staff; or to gain particular skills for the business.

Stretch Yourself Answers
1. On the basis of cost, efficiency and availability of skills.
2. A temporary expert may be more expensive but only needed for a short term. A permanent expert may only be needed now and again but could bring other benefits, for example knowledge of the businesses systems or the ability to train others.
3. Company pension schemes, provision of a company car, staff canteens, staff discounts, profit sharing and annual bonus payments.

Pages 48–49 Understanding Legislation
Test Yourself Answers
1. Employers must provide safe, healthy and comfortable working conditions, protection from danger in the workplace, breaks and holidays, and pay a fair rate for work done.
2. They should be on time, work to the best of their ability and do nothing to harm the business.
3. They must get equal recruitment, training and promotion opportunities.
4. The relationship between employer groups and employee groups such as Trades Unions.

Stretch Yourself Answers
1. Proper washroom and toilet facilities; ventilation; fire exits; safe levels of heating and lighting; guards fitted to dangerous machines.
2. Single union agreements are where all workers belong to the same Trade Union. This means they can negotiate from a strong position. Employers gain by only dealing with one body.
3. Because of the costs to both employer and employees.

Pages 50–51 Training and Performance Review
Test Yourself Answers
1. A training programme that introduces the worker to the workplace and the job, covering basic information and how the business works.
2. It increases the skills and knowledge of the worker and may also lead to additional qualifications.
3. A process that allows the employee to exchange views with the employer, usually in a formal or semi-formal setting.
4. They tend to focus on the employer's view and are often linked to Key Performance Indicators that benefit the business more than the employee.

Stretch Yourself Answers
1. The necessity for workers to keep retraining and learning new skills.
2. Because technology is constantly changing and new jobs and skills are always being needed. Businesses need trained staff in order to keep up with changes.
3. A trained worker will be more valuable to the business but will also be better able to get a job elsewhere.

Pages 52–53 Answers to Practice Questions
Answers to Knowledge Questions
1. Motivation
2. Staff retention
3. Remuneration
4. Minimum wage
5. Commission
6. Employment rights
7. HASAW
8. Induction training
9. Development
10. Appraisal

Answers to Application Questions
11. Flexible working gives the worker better use of their time (1), savings in travel (1) and freedom to organise work as they wish (1).
12. Motivation would arise because the worker is gaining something extra (1) that they would otherwise have to pay for. It is an additional benefit to their salary (1).

Answers to Analysis and Evaluation Questions
13. If 21st Century Tech employed a full-time expert, there would be no security issues (1) and s/he would have good knowledge of the system (1). S/he would also be able to train other people in the business up to the same level (1). However, they would be more expensive than a temporary worker (1) and their skills would be under-used for a big part of the year (1). A temporary worker would be cheaper (1) but would have to have security clearance (1).
Whatever decision you make, you must support it with reasons (3) such as: 'for this business, I think security is the most important factor, so I would appoint a permanent staff member'.

Operations

Pages 54–55 Methods of Production
Test Yourself Answers
1. Production describes the ways that raw materials and other inputs are turned into the final product, called output. It is the process involving inputs, transformation and outputs.
2. Where a product is a 'one-off' made to individual specifications.
3. Where the same inputs are used to produce different batches or groups of output.
4. Where each worker can specialise on a particular task. This makes them more efficient, but it may also demotivate them through boredom.

Stretch Yourself Answers
1. Being more efficient by reducing the amount of inputs, especially time.
2. Workers can be good and efficient at a certain task but can also be bored and lose interest. Boring and repetitive jobs can also be automated. This is good for the business's efficiency, but not for workers.
3. Sometimes changing the nature of the job helps. For example, job rotation moves the worker between jobs and job enrichment is used to make the job more interesting.

Pages 56–57 Business Expansion and Growth
Test Yourself Answers
1. For example in the number of products for sale, the range of products, or the size of its market share.
2. Growth from within at a gradual pace.
3. Joining with other businesses – integration.
4. Horizontal – businesses at the same stage of production; vertical – to a previous stage of production (backward) or a further stage (forward); lateral – to a similar but not directly related market; conglomerate (also called diversification) – to an unrelated area.
5. Financial; bulk buying; technical; risk bearing.

Stretch Yourself Answers
1. Consumers could gain from greater choice and lower prices as economies are passed on. Businesses can gain from economies of scale. Integration could mean that a business takes its competitors out of the market; the business could make more profit, but this would mean higher prices and less choice for the consumer.
2. Internal: retained profits, sale of unwanted assets. External: loans and share issues.

Pages 58–59 Managing and Maintaining Quality
Test Yourself Answers
1. Ones that do what they are supposed to do. In UK law, this means that they are fit for purpose.
2. Traditional quality control systems check quality at the end of production, so any faulty production is lost and inputs go to waste.
3. Every person involved in production is responsible for quality; checks for quality are made as the product enters an area, is processed and before it leaves. 'Total' also extends to parts, materials and other inputs.
4. Continuous improvement; everyone should see how their process could be made better so that many small changes can lead to big improvements in quality.

Stretch Yourself Answers
1. Costs need to be kept down to allow prices to remain competitive, but if quality is not maintained, there are likely to be costs in terms of damage to reputation, loss of customers and falling demand.
2. Choose three from ISO 9001, the kitemark symbol; the Customer Service Excellence Standard; the EFQM Excellence model; Investors in People.

Pages 60–61 Research and Good Design
Test Yourself Answers
1. It can make its products stand out from others by differentiating them, by good design and by branding.
2. Function refers to what the product actually does: aesthetic to how it looks.
3. An example could be a new drug or medicine. It doesn't matter what it looks like, but it is important that it works as it should.
4. An example could be a fashion item – something that is made to look good or unusual on the catwalk, but isn't necessarily practical to wear.
5. R&D tries to develop products that have the balance that will attract the customer to buy, based on the design mix of function, aesthetic and cost.

Stretch Yourself Answers
1. Through advertising or promotions that show the product in a good light, or make certain claims for it.
2. If people think of a particular branded product as having good design features, its reputation can be extended to other goods using the brand.

Pages 62–63 Managing Stock
Test Yourself Answers
1. Inventory.
2. This could be raw materials, partly finished goods, components, spares for machinery or stock of finished goods.
3. If stock is highly valuable, or perishable, or expensive to store.
4. Just-in-time (JIT) stock control plans for stock to arrive just as it is needed, so there are no storage costs. Just-in-case holds stock in case it is needed.

Stretch Yourself Answers

1. Those businesses running production lines or making products via processing; if there was a stock shortage, production would be unable to continue and other inputs could be lost.
2. Holding more stock than the minimum level needed by the business so that there is a buffer against a shortfall or a delay.

Pages 64–65 Answers to Practice Questions
Answers to Knowledge Questions
1. c) 2. c) 3. b) 4. d) 5. d) 6. b) 7. a) 8. d) 9. c) 10. a)

Answers to Application Questions
11. One that 'does what it is supposed to do' (2). It does not have to be expensive (1).
12. Kernels will use batch production (1), both in the production of the chocolates and in making different-sized boxes (1). Batch production uses the same machinery and processes (1) to produce different batches of goods (1). It also uses job production (1) in the making of its specialist chocolate fountains as these are made to order (1).
13. There are likely to be costs in terms of damage to reputation (1), loss of customers (1) and falling demand (1) if quality is not maintained.

Answers to Analysis and Evaluation Questions
14. Consumers could gain from greater choice (1) and lower prices (1), if lower costs (1) are passed on (1), or it could mean less competition (1) if Holborn reduces consumer choice (1) and charges higher prices (1) to make more profit (1).
15. The type of integration proposed is horizontal integration (1), as it involves two businesses at the same stage of production (1) and in the same industry (1). This could bring benefits of greater efficiency (1) from economies of scale (1) and lower costs, so lower prices (1).
16. For example, if you decide that the merger should go ahead, you could talk about the four possible economies of scale, with examples of each linked to these businesses, so such as financial (1) – lenders giving better rates (1); bulk buying (1) – buying chocolate ingredients at lower prices (1); technical economies (1) such as using specialist machines and workers (1) and risk-bearing economies (1), as risk is spread over more products and markets (1).
    You should balance this against possible diseconomies of scale, such as longer chains of communication (1), particularly between Holborn and Kernels (1), more remote management at Holborn (1) and different production processes (1).

Finance and Accounts

Pages 66–67 Obtaining Finance
Test Yourself Answers
1. Choose three from: at start-up, to buy materials, to pay for power or fuel, to buy or rent equipment and premises; later, to pay wages and suppliers and to advertise that they are open for business, also to grow and to compete.
2. The owner's funds.
3. Through the Business Start Up Scheme or charities like The Prince's Youth Business Trust.
4. Trade credit; hire purchase; leasing.
5. Formal, such as loans and mortgages; informal, such as spreading of payments.

Stretch Yourself Answers
1. For example retained profit or sale of unwanted assets.
2. Overdrafts, loans and mortgages.

Pages 68–69 Revenues, Costs and Breakeven
Test Yourself Answers
1. Costs that do not vary with output and are paid regardless of production, such as rent.
2. Indirect costs; another name for fixed costs is overheads.
3. Costs that vary directly with output, such as parts, power and ingredients.
4. The point at which the business is making neither a profit nor a loss. It is measured as total cost = total revenue.
5. The formula is: 1) Price per unit – variable cost per unit = contribution to fixed costs; 2) Fixed costs ÷ total contribution = breakeven level of sales.

Stretch Yourself Answers
1. If a business makes several products, it can be difficult to say which costs are which, or which particular product is making or losing money.
2. The cost of the time and expertise of the owners.

Pages 70–71 Understanding Accounts
Test Yourself Answers
1. Stakeholders use it to make comparisons and judge progress; managers use it to plan for the future.
2. The amount it costs to make or produce a product – raw materials, components, stock, etc.
3. Wages, rent and power.
4. Increasing efficiency, raising revenue or cutting costs.
5. Because customers might reduce the amount they buy, leading to a fall in revenue.

Stretch Yourself Answers
1. How easily a business can pay its short-term debts from its assets.
2. (Operating) profit ÷ sales × 100, to give a percentage; it shows how much profit is being made per £1 of sales.
3. This is to do with the nature of the business. Some businesses have very high turnover, so make just a little profit on many sales. Others have low turnover, so need to make more profit on each sale.

Pages 72–73 Using the Balance Sheet
Test Yourself Answers
1. It shows what the business owns as against what it owes. It therefore measures assets (owns) against liabilities (owes).
2. Because the two sides are measuring the same thing.
3. Non-current assets are those which it is harder to turn into cash, such as land, buildings and machinery used in production. Current assets are those that are easier to turn into cash.
4. Current liabilities are debts that must be paid back within a year, like bank overdrafts or creditors. Non-current liabilities, like mortgages and long-term loans, have more than a year before they must be repaid.

Stretch Yourself Answers
1. The current and acid test ratios.
2. Assets minus liabilities gives what the business is worth at this moment. This is called net current assets.
3. How the money for net current assets was raised, for example shareholders' funds, profit, or profit made in previous periods (reserves).

Pages 74–75 Managing Cashflow
Test Yourself Answers
1. The money flowing into and out of a business.
2. Cash comes in through sales revenue and flows out to pay for costs.
3. A cashflow forecast looks at predicted flows of cash in and out of the business and shows the business when it will be short of cash, or have a cash surplus, so that it can plan.
4. Spreading payments, such as making monthly payments; or rescheduling payments – paying a bill at a later date.
5. Arranging to receive revenue more regularly; or arranging to receive payments early.

Stretch Yourself Answers
1. A cash surplus is where there is more cash coming in than the business needs; a cash shortage or deficit is where there is less cash than it needs.
2. Because excess cash does not earn any return; if a business is holding a lot of cash, it is losing the opportunity to gain a return with it.

Pages 76–77 Answers to Practice Questions
Answers to Knowledge Questions
1. c) 2. d) 3. c) 4. a) 5. c) 6. d) 7. b) 8. c) 9. d) 10. c)

Answers to Application Questions
11. Costs include raw materials (1), such as paper and ink (1) and the costs of the vans (1) – petrol, licences, etc. (1). Other costs are power (1), the premises, e.g. rent and rates (1), employee wages (1), for example the driver (1) and Ali and Eddie's own wages (1). Their revenues come from the businesses for which they do the printing (1).
12. They could have used owner's funds (1), a bank loan (1), a bank overdraft (1) or a grant from government or a charity like the Prince's Trust (1).
13. Profitability ratios compare the amount of profit made with revenue (2). They show how much profit is being made per £ of revenue (1). It is important for Kwyk-Print to know that their ratio is acceptable for the business they are in (1).

Answers to Analysis and Evaluation Questions

14. Breakeven will be of little use, because the business makes a number of different products (1) at different prices (1). It would therefore be difficult to say exactly how much each costs (1). The business could use the contribution (1) method to see which products are contributing most to breakeven.(1)
15. Kwyk-Print could decide to hold less stock of paper and inks (1), could persuade customers to pay in advance (1) or arrange to pay its own bills later (1). It could also spread payments for power, vehicle insurance, etc. (1). Any efficiency savings could also help (1).
16. Borrowing from a friend would be cheap (1) and certain (1) and immediate (1), but they would hand over some of the control of the business (1). Borrowing from the bank means a formal agreement (1) and payment of interest (1). The machine is put at risk if secured on the bank (1). There is no 'right' answer (often the case in business studies). Four marks are awarded for judgements that are made and supported by argument.

Understanding the Context of Business

Pages 78–79 Different Types of Market
Test Yourself Answers
1. Demand is the amount a customer is willing to pay at a price. Supply is the amount a business is willing to sell at that price. As price rises, demand tends to fall and supply tends to rise. Where the two meet is where the market agrees on price, called price equilibrium.
2. Ones having lots of businesses that cannot compete on price, so instead compete through better customer service, branding and advertising.
3. A market in which there is little competition; a monopoly in the UK is defined as a business with 25 per cent market share.
4. These could include legal barriers, like patents; restrictive practices, like agreeing prices with suppliers; the amount of initial investment needed; high advertising spend and strong brands.
5. Crops and raw materials produced in bulk that have one worldwide price. Small businesses rely on commodities but have no control over their price.

Stretch Yourself Answers
1. They try to make their products or services unique, brand themselves and use advertising and promotion.
2. Each of these tactics has a cost, so may lead to higher prices. Customers may then choose to go elsewhere.

Pages 80–81 Global Competition
Test Yourself Answers
1. Countries can exchange goods that they are able to produce with those that other countries produce.
2. Visibles are goods, invisibles are services. If Country A sells a product to Country B, this is an export from A and an import into B.
3. A business that has operations in many countries.
4. Companies that hold shares in other companies in the same group so they are part of a global brand but can keep their local or national identities.

Stretch Yourself Answers
1. Globalisation describes how competition in many industries is now on a global scale, rather than just national.
2. Global businesses can produce in countries with cheaper labour and pay tax in countries with lower tax, which can give them a poor reputation. They can also keep costs down. Global brands mean consumers get the same quality for the same good anywhere in the world, but if local businesses cannot compete, consumer choice is reduced.
3. They may be able to take advantage of poorer countries, operate in places with lower labour costs, less strict labour laws, fewer rules and regulations or lower tax, exploit labour or natural resources. They have been accused of destroying the environment and even of political interference.

Pages 82–83 Ethical and Environmental Issues
Test Yourself Answers
1. Doing the right or moral thing, such as not testing products on animals and not using cheap or child labour.
2. Not doing anything that might harm the planet or its wildlife. An example is sustainable production, where businesses always put back into the environment at least as much as they have taken out.
3. The ethical and environmental policies of businesses.
4. Social costs are problems carried by society as a whole, for example pollution or congestion. Social benefits are gains shared by everyone, for example recreation facilities.

Stretch Yourself Answers
1. They attract customers who want to be ethical and 'green', and these customers stay loyal to the business. Green policies like recycling and green fuels may actually cut costs, but businesses can often charge higher prices for 'green' products, bringing higher profits.
2. Groups of people or organisations who try to influence businesses and governments to act in ethical or environmental ways.

Pages 84–85 Government and EU Influence
Test Yourself Answers
1. These include government spending, taxation and laws to protect workers.
2. Taxes on consumers affect demand. VAT affects price. Taxes on business profits may also have an effect.
3. A market comprising the total population of all EU nations, which is available to all businesses within EU states.

Stretch Yourself Answers
1. Most businesses rely on credit of some sort, or on overdrafts or loans, so higher interest rates increase their costs. Many consumers have debt, for example mortgages, so higher interest rates reduce their ability to spend.
2. Three from: minimum wage; maximum working hours; the right to join a trades union; equal treatment for men and women; worker involvement in business; freedom to work anywhere in the EU.

Pages 86–87 External Economic Influences
Test Yourself Answers
1. Those factors that are outside of the control of the business.
2. It depends on the market in which the business operates, for example a business running old people's homes would benefit from an ageing population, but one selling teenage fashions might suffer.
3. High levels of consumer spending and low levels of unemployment. At the top of the boom, there will be rising wages and rising prices. Businesses will find it harder to meet increased demand and prices will rise.
4. Production and expenditure in an economy: positive growth means strong demand; negative or zero growth means weak demand.

Stretch Yourself Answers
1. It affects the price of imports and exports, making them more or less expensive as it changes.
2. They change the prices of certain goods and services; when the value of the pound goes up and down, so does the price of imports and exports.
3. At the initial exchange rate, the grocer would need £50 to buy €80. At the new rate, this is now £53.33 (80 ÷ 1.5).

Pages 88–89 Answers to Practice Questions
Answers to Knowledge Questions

1. market	2. 25 per cent	3. social costs
4. commodities	5. invisible	6. multinationals
7. corporate social responsibility	8. pressure groups	9. demand
10. recession		

Answers to Application Questions
11. Being ethical means doing the right or moral thing (1). An ethical policy is one that shows that this is what the business does (1). An example for Baseline could be not buying raw materials extracted by child labour (2).
12. Baseline brings in materials (visible imports) (1) and sells sets abroad (visible exports) (1). It also sells a service package (invisible export) (1).
13. Baseline operates in a competitive market (1). This means lots of businesses (1), and such competition tends to bring lower prices (1). There is also more consumer choice (1).

Answers to Analysis and Evaluation Questions
14. Carbon footprint is the amount of carbon (1), and therefore environmental damage (1), released through producing sets (1). Baseline could use more recycled inputs (1), recycle its own waste (1), only use materials from sustainable sources (1), control pollution (1), use greener fuels (1) or adopt energy saving policies.
15. Being ethical and environmentally responsible can bring advantages of greater efficiency (1) and lower costs (1). For example, recycled inputs (1) are likely to be cheaper (1), energy-saving policies save money (1) and better fuel efficiency saves money (1). Baseline also gets a better reputation (1) and more loyal customers (1).

Index